If
Only
He
Knew

If Only He Knew

Gary Smalley
with Steve Scott

R. M. Marketing
1050 Valley Forge Plaza
King of Prussia, Pennsylvania 19406

To the number one woman in my life —
Norma Jean
and to our children,
Kari, Greg, and Michael

THE AUTHORS

Gary Smalley has been researching, lecturing, and counseling on marriage and family life for 16 years. He is responsible for the direction and content of the book. His co-author, Steven Scott, a free-lance writer, is responsible for its composition.

SPECIAL THANKS

Bonney Scott: For her loving commitment which made the scheduled completion of this book possible.

Robert J. Marsh: For his vision and encouragement, without which this book would not have been written for at least three years.

The Principals of R.M. Marketing:
For their courage in committing the financial resources that made our dream a reality.

Harry Howard: For coordinating the layout and physical production of this book.

The Editorial Staff: Judy Baggett Thrasher and Linda Allen Fyke for enabling us to complete a two-year project in two months.

The Typists: Anna Ruth Hart, Betty Snyder, Lisa Bland, Darlene Williams, Janet Perry, and Denise Duck; for working your fingers to the bone.

A NOTE FROM THE AUTHOR'S WIFE

In our continuing work with couples, Gary and I have come to one conclusion: there is no such thing as a totally unique problem. In fact, most couples are usually relieved to know their problems are common to many, if not all couples. Because marital problems can be so similar, you find a solution that works with several couples, it usually turns out to be equally effective for most couples.

Please rest assured you are not the first husband in the history of humanity to experience the problems you are facing. The principles that Gary shares in this book have not only made our marriage more fulfilling, but they have had similar results in the lives of countless other couples with whom we have worked. As you begin to apply these principles to your relationship, you should begin to experience a deeper and richer marriage.

Norma Smalley

CONTENTS

IF ONLY I KNEW

Before I approached Gary about writing a "marriage book for men," I knew his material was good, but I had no idea how meaningful it would be to me personally. After all, I had been married for almost ten years and I was nearly an "ideal husband". . .I thought. As I began to work with Gary on the material for this book, it became more and more clear that I was not a successful husband by any stretch of the imagination. I was providing for my wife's material needs, and some of her physical needs, but that's where it stopped.

As I got deeper into the content, I realized that for years I had been unaware of many of my wife's emotional needs. For years, she had to put up with a husband whose callousness and indifference forced her to suffer through day after day of not having her deeper needs lovingly satisfied. I am extremely grateful for all that I have learned in the past two months. At last my eyes have been opened and I see my wife as the unique, beautiful individual that she really is. I am devoting the rest of my life to becoming the husband she deserves. The content of this book not only opened my eyes to my wife and her needs, but it gave me concrete ways to meet them. If you get one-tenth the value from this book that I have gleaned from its pages, it will be the most valuable book you'll ever read on marriage.

Steve Scott

How to drive your wife away without even trying

At the other end of the phone a quivering voice said, "You've got to help me. She has a court order against me." George was coming to me for help after his relationship with his wife was already in shreds. "We've been married over twenty years and she won't even let me back in the house. I can't believe she would treat me this way after all I've done for her. Can you help us get back together?"

Before I answered his question, I wanted to talk to his wife. "There's no way you can talk to Barbara," he said. "She wouldn't talk to you. The moment you say you're representing me in any way, she'll hang up on you."

"I've never been turned down by a wife yet," I assured him, "so we might as well see if this will be the first time. Would you give me her phone number?"

To be honest, as grim as things sounded, I did wonder if she would be the first wife not willing to talk to me about her marital strife. But my doubts were unfounded — she was more than anxious to discuss their problems.

"What would it take for you to be willing to let your husband back into your life? What would have to happen before you would try to rebuild a marriage relationship with him?" Those were the same questions I asked many wives who claimed they didn't want their husbands back.

Her response was typical, "I can't possibly answer that

question. He's the worst husband in the world. So I wouldn't think of taking him back. I can't stand his personality or his offensive habits anymore." The court order would take care of him, she told me. "Just keep him away!"

I gently asked her if she could tell me the things he had done to offend her. When I heard her response, I said, "It sounds like he hasn't been a very sensitive and gentle husband, has he?"

Once again I asked her to stretch her imagination and think about what changes would be necessary to take him back.

There was plenty of room for improvement, she told me. First, he was too domineering and critical of her. Second, he tried to control her every move with a possessive grip. Third, he trampled her sense of selfworth with constant ridicule. And fourth, although he always had time for business and other interests, he seldom took time to listen to her. On top of all that, he spied on her and didn't give her any freedom, she said.

"Don't get any ideas, though," she told me at the end of our conversation, "because no matter what, I won't stop the divorce."

When I relayed these complaints to George, I knew I had touched some sensitive spots. He defended himself and accused her. I let him rant for awhile before asking, "Do you want your wife back?"

"Yes, I'd do anything," he said.

"Good, I'm always willing to work with someone ready to readjust his life. But if you're not totally serious, let me know now. I don't like to play games." Again he committed himself to change but his commitment didn't last beyond my next statement. "We're going to have to work on your domineering and possessive nature. It shows you don't genuinely love your wife."

He fumed and spouted, defended and fought so much I began to wonder if he really would commit himself to the necessary changes.

"I've never met a more belligerent, stubborn man in my entire life!" I exclaimed.

Suddenly subdued, he responded, "That's not my nature, I'm usually rather submissive inside. Maybe I'm putting up a front because I'm really not a pushy person. I feel like people run all over me."

"I don't think you and I are talking about the same person," I responded, "If I were your wife, I'm not sure I could bear up emotionally under your domineering personality."

That stopped him long enough to give our conversation some serious thought. After talking to his friends and even praying about his problem, he returned, able to confess his faults and ready to change.

"If you really want to love your wife, then you need to begin right now, at the divorce trial," I said. Now that we were on the subject, he mentioned he needed to get a lawyer because she had one.

"No," I cautioned him, "If you want to win her back, you need to forget about a lawyer at this time." (I don't always recommend this, but based on their personal background, I felt he would stand a better chance of regaining her love without legal counsel.)

"You're crazy," he said. "They'll take me to the cleaners."

Feeling somewhat defenseless, he reluctantly agreed to forfeit legal counsel.

Two of his friends and I waited in the courthouse for the closed-room session to end. He came running out of the courtroom bellowing, "She wants twenty percent of my retirement. . .twenty percent! No way I'm gonna do that!"

Once again I asked him, "Do you want your wife back?" Again, he nodded yes! "Then give her twenty-five percent." I reminded him that *now* was the time to respect her and treat her sensitively. Later, he emerged from the closed doors a divorced man, but not for long. . .

Several months later I ran into him at the grocery store. "My wife and I remarried," he said triumphantly. "I thought you were crazy when you first told me the things I should do for my wife. There was no way I would ever be able to do them," he continued. "It took sheer willpower. I only did them because you said I should. But you know, it's really amazing, after doing them for three months, I actually enjoy them."

He gave an example of the new way he treated his wife. Once when she took a business trip, he wrote her a note telling her how much he wished he could be with her. Inserted in the note were extra money and directions on how to reach her destination.

He finally realized his wife is a special person who needs tender treatment, almost as if her forehead were stamped "Handle With Care!"

When I called seeking permission to use their case history in my book, she was baking a birthday cake for him. She seemed very happy with her "new" husband and the sensitivity he has developed.

TWO BIG REASONS MARRIAGES FAIL

1. *Entering marriage with "storyland" expectations and limited training.*

I once asked a college girl what kind of man she would like to marry. "I'd like for him to be able to tell jokes, sing and dance, and stay home at night."

"You don't want a husband," I told her. "You want a television set."

Her visions of a husband reveal one of the most common reasons marriages fail. We marry with unrealistic expectations and little or no skills to take care of our mates. In fact, most of us are rather "fuzzy-headed" when it comes to our mate's real needs. Isn't it ironic that a plumber's license requires four years of training, but a marriage license requires nothing but two willing bodies and sometimes a blood test. Since most of us bounce through the educational corridors without any basic communication courses, many men marry with absolutely no knowledge of how to fulfill the emotional and mental needs of a woman.

Recently I asked five divorced women, individually, "If your husband began treating you in a consistently loving manner, would you take him back?"

"Of course I would," each replied. But unfortunately, none had hope that her husband would ever be like that.

Because I knew one of the men personally, I had to concur with his wife's hopelessness. If he were willing to try, he could win her back. Unfortunately, he wasn't interested in learning.

"What he doesn't realize is that a lot of women are as responsive as puppy dogs," one woman explained to me. "If he'd come back and treat me with tenderness, gentleness and understanding, I'd take him back tomorrow."

How sad that we men don't know how to win our wives back or even how to keep from losing them. How can we win their affection, their respect, their love and cooperation when we don't even know where to begin? Instead of trying to mend a cracked marriage, most of us would rather jump on the divorce bandwagon.

When we violate the relationship laws inherent in marriage, we wonder why it all went sour. But you wouldn't wonder if the law of aerodynamics sent a one-winged airplane plummeting to the earth.

Imagine yourself an aerospace engineer working for NASA. Your job is to put several men on the moon, but something goes wrong halfway through their flight. You wouldn't dream of walking out on the entire project because something went wrong. Instead, you and the other engineers would put your heads together, insert data into the computer and. . .voila! You would discover the problem and make all the vital adjustments to get that spacecraft back on course. If the project had failed altogether, you wouldn't forsake it. You would simply modify it to avoid similar problems in the future.

Like the spacecraft, your marriage is subject to laws that determine its success or failure. If any of these laws are violated, you and your wife are locked into orbits, destined to crash. However, if during the marriage you recognize which law or principle you are violating and make the necessary adjustments, I believe your marriage will stay on the right course.

2. *Lack of understanding about the general differences between men and women.*

I would venture to say that most marital difficulties center around one fact — men and women are TOTALLY different. The differences (emotionally, mentally and physically) are so extreme that without a *concentrated effort* to understand them, it is nearly impossible to have a happy marriage. A world-renowned psychiatrist once said, "After thirty years of studying women, I ask myself, 'What is it that they really want?' " If this was his conclusion after exhaustive study, just imagine how little you know about your wife.

You may already be aware of some of the differences. Many,

however, will come as a complete surprise. Did you know, for instance, that virtually every cell in a man's body has a chromosome makeup entirely different than those in a woman's body? How about this next one? Dr. James Dobson says there is strong evidence indicating that the "seat" of the emotions in a man's brain is wired differently than in the woman's. By virtue of these two differences, men and women are miles apart emotionally and physically. Let's examine some more of the general differences between men and women.

GENERAL MENTAL/EMOTIONAL DIFFERENCES

1. Women tend to be more *"personal"* than men. Women seem to be more interested in people and feelings, while men are more preoccupied with subjects and things that can be discussed via logic and reasoning.

2. Dr. Cecil Osborne, in his book *The Art of Understanding Your Mate,* said women become *an intimate part of* the people they know and the things that surround them; they enter into a kind of "oneness" with their environment. Though a man relates to people and situations, he usually doesn't allow his identity to become entwined with them. He somehow remains apart. That's why a woman, viewing her house as an extension of herself, can be hurt when it's criticized by others. We might explain this difference by comparing a man to a paintbrush and a woman to the paint. Though the brush touches the entire canvas, it finally comes to rest on the pallet. The paint, on the other hand, enters into a *oneness* with the canvas and can only be separated from it at great cost.

3. Because of a woman's emotional identity with the people and places around her, she needs more time to adjust to change than a man. He can logically deduce the benefits of a change and get "psyched-up" for it in a matter of minutes. Not so with a woman. Since she focuses on immediate consequences of a change, she needs time to overcome the initial adjustment before warming up to the advantages of it.

GENERAL PHYSICAL DIFFERENCES

Dr. Paul Popenoe, founder of the American Institute of Family Relations in Los Angeles, has dedicated his most productive years to the research of biological differences between the sexes. Some of his findings are listed below:

• Women have greater constitutional vitality, perhaps because of their unique chromosome makeup. Normally, females in the U.S. outlive males by three or four years.

• A woman's metabolism is normally lower than a man's.

• Men and women differ in skeletal structure, the woman having a shorter head, broader face, less protruding chin, shorter legs, and longer trunk. The first finger of a woman's hand is usually longer than the third; with men the reverse is true. Boys' teeth usually last longer than girls'.

• Woman has larger kidneys, liver, stomach and appendix than man, but smaller lungs.

• Women have several very important functions lacking in men: menstruation, pregnancy, lactation. Women's hormones are of a different type and more numerous than men's. These hormonal differences influence behavior and feelings.

• The woman's thyroid is larger and more active. It enlarges during pregnancy and menstruation; makes her more prone to goiter; provides resistance to cold; is associated with the smooth skinned, relatively hairless body, and thick layer of subcutaneous fat (an important factor in the concept of personal beauty).

• A woman's blood contains more water (20% fewer red cells). Since the red cells supply oxygen to the body cells, she tires more easily and is more prone to faint. Her constitutional vitality is, therefore, strictly limited to "life span". When the working day in British factories was increased from ten to twelve hours, accidents among women increased 150% but not at all among men.

• On the average, men possess 50% more brute strength than women.

• Women's hearts beat more rapidly (80 beats per minute vs. 72 for men). Her blood pressure (10 points lower than man) varies from minute to minute, but she has less tendency toward high blood pressure — at least until after menopause.

- Her vital capacity or breathing power is significantly lower.
- She withstands high temperatures better than a man because her metabolism slows down less.

GENERAL DIFFERENCES IN SEXUAL MOTIVATIONS

A woman's sexual drive tends to be related to her menstrual cycles, while a man's drive is fairly constant.

Women are stimulated more by touch and romantic words. They are far more attracted by a man's personality, while men are stimulated by sight. A man is usually less discriminating about those to whom he is physically attracted.

Women's fantasies usually revolve around persons they admire. They're more interested in a romantic, long-term relationship than mere experiences. That's why you rarely read of women raping men.

While a man needs little or no preparation for sex, a woman often needs hours of emotional and mental preparation. Harsh or abusive treatment can easily remove her desire for sexual intimacy for days at a time. When a woman's emotions have been trampled by her husband, she is often repulsed by his advances. Many women have told me they feel like prostitutes when they're forced to make love while feeling resentment toward their husbands. However, a man may have NO idea what he is putting his wife through when he forces sex upon her.

These basic differences, which usually surface soon after the wedding, are the source of many conflicts in marriage. From the start, the woman has a greater intuitive awareness of how to develop a loving relationship. Because of her sensitivity, she is initially more considerate of his feelings and enthusiastic about developing a meaningful, multi-level relationship. That is, she knows how to build something more than a sexual marathon. She wants to be a lover, a best friend, a fan, a homemaker, and an appreciated partner. The man, on the other hand, does not generally have her instinctive awareness of what the relationship should be. He doesn't know how to encourage and love his wife or treat her in a way that meets her deepest needs.

Since he doesn't have an understanding of these vital areas through intuition, he must rely *solely* upon the knowledge and skills he has acquired *prior* to marriage. Unfortunately, our educational system does not require a training program for a husband-to-be. His only education may be the example he observed in his home. For most of us, that example was insufficient. We enter marriage knowing everything about sex and very little about genuine, unselfish love.

I am not saying men are more selfish than women. I'm simply saying at the outset of a marriage, I believe a husband is not as equally equipped to *express* unselfish love as his wife.

GENERAL DIFFERENCES IN
INTUITIVE KNOWLEDGE AND SKILLS

Norman was planning to invest more than $50,000 in a business opportunity that was a "sure thing". He had scrutinized it from every angle and logically deducted it couldn't miss. After signing a contract and delivering a check to the other party, he decided to tell his wife about the investment.

Upon hearing a few of the details, she immediately felt uneasy about the deal. He sensed her uneasiness and became angry, asking why she felt that way. She couldn't give a logical reason because she didn't have one. All she knew was that it just didn't "sit right". Norman gave in and went back to the other party, asking for a refund. "You're Crazy!" the man told him as he returned Norman's money. A short time later, ALL of the organizers and investors were indicted by the federal government. His wife's intuition had not only saved him $50,000, but it may have kept him out of jail.

What exactly is "woman's intuition"? It's not something mystical. According to a Stanford University research team led by neuro-psychologists McGuinness and Tribran, women do catch subliminal messages faster and more accurately than men. Since this intuition is based on an unconscious mental process, many women aren't able to give specific explanations for the way they feel. They simply perceive or "feel" a situation or person, while men tend to follow a logical analysis of *circumstances* or *people*.

Now that you know WHY men and women cannot understand their respective differences without great effort, I hope you will have more hope, patience, and tolerance as you endeavor to strengthen and deepen your relationship with your wife. With this in mind, we're ready to look at some of the serious consequences of allowing a poor marriage to continue in its downhill slide.

SERIOUS CONSEQUENCES OF A POOR MARRIAGE

First, a woman who is not properly loved by her husband can develop any number of serious physical ailments needing thousands of dollars worth of treatment, according to Dr. Ed Wheat in his tapes on sexual harmony in marriage. Every aspect of a woman's emotional and physical existence is dependent on the romantic love she receives from her husband, Dr. James Dobson said, so husbands, if *you* feel locked out of your bedroom, listen closely now. According to Dr. Dobson, when a man learns to love his wife in the way she needs to be loved, she will respond to him physically in a way he never dreamed possible.

Secondly, a husband's lack of love for his wife can drastically affect their children's emotional development, according to John Drescher in his book, *Seven Things Children Need*.

Third, a rebellious wife and child are more likely to be found in the home of a man who does not know how to lovingly support his family. This is discussed in greater detail in Chapter Five.

Fourth, when a man settles for a poor marriage, he is forfeiting his reputation before all the world. He is saying, "I don't care what I promised at the marriage altar, I'm not going to try any longer." By refusing to love his wife as he should, he is telling those around him he is self-centered and unreliable.

Fifth, his son will probably learn many of the wrong ways to treat his future wife by modeling after his father. Unloving parents simply can't keep their problems to themselves. They are bound to affect their children's future relationships.

Sixth, improper love increases the possibility of mental illness requiring psychiatric treatment of family members. According to an article in Family Weekly, July 16, 1978, Dr. Nathan Ackerman says mental illness originates within a family and is transmitted from generation to generation. In that same article a psychiatrist from Philadelphia, Dr. Salvador Minuchin, says family members often get caught in a groove of mental illness by putting undue stress on each other.

THE HARDEST DECISION YOU MAY EVER MAKE

You may feel it's impossible to change lifelong habits. But I hope you still decide to try. I know from experience the rewards are well worth the effort.

I am not trying to force you into the "perfect husband mold". I don't know *any* perfect husbands, but I do know some who are learning how to respond to their wives' special needs. I want to help you learn how to love your wife more effectively. At first you may feel like you're learning to walk all over again. Weeks, months or even a couple of years may pass before you reach your goal of consistent loving behavior. After you learn to toddle slowly, you will gain confidence. Soon you will be walking boldly, then running, and then leaping right into the kind of marriage you never thought possible.

Remember that *you* are the one who gains when you strive to have a loving relationship with your wife. My wife Norma has told me dozens of times that when I treat her right I'm the one who wins. My loving care motivates her to do extra things for me, to respond gladly to my needs and desires.

My wife and I have committed the remaining years of our lives to study skills needed to rebuild meaningful relationships. I have personally interviewed hundreds of women about their husbands' actions that tear down or build up their marriages. Basically, this book is a summary of my findings.

Your wife may be a career woman without children or a busy homemaker and mother of three. Whatever the case, I believe you can *customize* the general principles in this book to build a more fulfilling relationship with her.

Before reading the next chapter, take this short quiz to rate how stable your marriage is at this moment. Then, when you have pinpointed your weak and strong points, use the chapters that follow to take steps necessary to strengthen your relationship. Some of the ideas for this checklist are from Dr. George Larson of Arizona, a psychologist who has done extensive work helping people develop good relationships. He believes, as I do, that good relationships don't just happen. They evolve and are sustained only when people know what they want and how to get it.

Answer YES or NO to each question, then check your score below:

1. Do you make your wife feel good about herself? (yes_____no_____)
2. Do you value the same things in your wife that you value in yourself? (yes_____no_____)
3. Does your face spontaneously break into a smile when you see your wife? (yes_____no_____)
4. When you leave the house, does your wife have a sense of well-being, having been nourished by your company? (yes_____no_____)
5. Can you and your wife tell each other honestly what you really want instead of using manipulation or games? (yes_____no_____)
6. Can your wife get angry at you without your thinking less of her? (yes_____no_____)
7. Can you accept your wife as she is instead of having several plans to re-do her? (yes_____no_____)
8. Is your behavior consistent with your words? (yes_____no_____)
9. Do your actions show you really care for your wife? (yes_____no_____)
10. Can you feel comfortable with your wife when she's wearing old clothes? (yes_____no_____)
11. Do you enjoy introducing your wife to your friends or acquaintances? (yes_____no_____)
12. Are you able to share with your wife your moments of weakness, failure, disappointments? (yes_____no_____)
13. Would your wife say you are a good listener? (yes_____no_____)
14. Do you trust your wife to solve her own problems? (yes_____no_____)
15. Do you admit to your wife you have problems and need her comfort? (yes_____no_____)

16. Do you believe you could live a full and happy life without your wife? (yes_____no_____)

17. Do you encourage your wife to develop her full potential as a woman? (yes_____no_____)

18. Are you able to learn from your wife and value what she says? (yes_____no_____)

19. If your wife were to die tomorrow, would you be very happy you had a chance to meet her and to marry her? (yes_____no_____)

20. Does your wife feel she's more important than anyone or anything else in your life? (yes_____no_____)

21. Do you believe you know at least five of your wife's major needs and how to meet those needs in a skillful way? (yes_____no_____)

22. Do you know what your wife needs when she's under stress or when she's discouraged? (yes_____no_____)

23. When you offend your wife, do you usually admit you were wrong and seek her forgiveness? (yes_____no_____)

24. Would your wife say you praise her at least once a day? (yes_____no_____)

25. Would your wife say you are open to her correction? (yes_____no_____)

26. Would your wife say you are a protector, that you know what her limitations are as a woman? (yes_____no_____)

27. Would your wife say you usually consider her feelings and ideas whenever making a major decision that affects the family or her? (yes_____no_____)

28. Would your wife say you enjoy being with her and sharing many of life's experiences with her? (yes_____no_____)

29. Would your wife say you are a good example of what you would like her to be? (yes_____no_____)

30. Would you say you create interest in her when you share things you consider important? (yes_____no_____)

SCORING

If you answered "yes" to *10 or less* questions, then your relationship is in major need of overhaul.

If you answered "yes" to *11 - 19* of the questions, your relationship needs improvement.

If you answered "yes" to *20 or more*, then you're probably on your way to a good lasting relationship.

2

Where have all the feelings gone?

"I don't love you anymore," Sandi said casually, shocking Jim out of his intense interest in a baseball game on TV. "I want to leave you and I'm taking Jamey with me," she added. He whirled around in his chair, wondering if he had heard correctly.

Since Sandi and Jim believed themselves to be sensible, educated adults, they separated calmly and agreed on a settlement without dispute. Jim, in his "maturity," even helped Sandi pack. Then he calmly watched as she and his daughter left his house for good. But he wasn't calm on the inside. He couldn't keep food down for the next month and it wasn't long before he developed shingles and boils. His physical problems were only symptoms of a much deeper problem — a lack of knowledge about how to build a lasting marriage relationship.

Fortunately, Jim was able to win his wife back in time with genuine love. After a year, Sandi was convinced by the changes in her husband that their marriage deserved another try.

Just what did Jim learn about love during a year of separation from Sandi? He learned that a successful marriage, like any other worthwhile endeavor, takes time and study.

Who would think of allowing an untrained man to climb into the cockpit of an airplane and tinker with the gauges? Or who would allow a novice to service the engines of a modern jet? Yet we expect men to build strong, loving relationships without any education at all. Most men don't have the slightest idea how to read the complicated "gauges" of a woman. A man first must discover the essentials of genuine love, then practice them until his skills are sharp and natural. Soon the awkwardness will give way to masterful ability.

Remember the couple I mentioned in the first chapter? By the time the husband finally asked me how he could win his wife's love back, she had already obtained a court order to keep him away from the house. The divorce was pending, although he desperately wanted to salvage their marriage of many years. I can remember telling him "It'll be difficult. But I assure you, as long as she isn't in love with another man, what I'm going to share with you will work."

At first, he felt awkward using the techniques I shared with him. He had to begin at zero and slowly learn to talk to his wife, to be tender, and to care about her feelings. He didn't know her special needs, that she longed for comfort and not lectures when discouraged. But in time, he DID learn and he DID win back his wife. He said he couldn't believe the gestures that once felt so awkward were now an enjoyable part of his life.

"It's just not worth it," one husband said when I told him how to save his marriage." "Don't you see, I don't like her anymore. She bugs me and I don't even want to make the effort to build what you're talking about. I just want out."

"What is the matter between the two of you?" I asked, trying to find out why his love for her had vanished. "Why can't you extend yourself toward her and try to build a loving relationship? Why don't you want to?"

"Well, several things she has done," he confided, "have hurt me so much that I just can't try anymore."

The next day at lunch he named seven things his wife had done and continued to do, that made him feel like leaving. To his amazement, we were able to trace each one of them to a lack of certain qualities in his life. Once he understood this, he asked, "What kind of man would I be to dump her when I'm contributing to the way she is?"

A marital relationship that endures and becomes more fulfilling for both the husband and the wife is no accident. Only hard work makes a marriage more fulfilling five, ten, fifteen or twenty years after the honeymoon. I enjoy my wife's company more than ever, and I'm looking forward to a deeper relationship in later years.

THE THREE ESSENTIAL KINDS OF LOVE

Nearly everyone enters marriage believing his love for his mate will never fade. Yet in the U.S. for every two marriages, there is one divorce. For too long we have grasped for "Hollywood's" version of love. It doesn't take long to discover that mere passion which revolves around sexual gratification is not sufficient, in itself, to establish a lasting relationship. Unfortunately, too many couples begin their marriages thinking this type of love is all they need.

There are at least three kinds of love, each totally unique. Of the three types of love — companionship, passion, and genuine love — I believe only the latter provides an adequate foundation for a secure relationship. If a relationship lacks genuine love, it will most likely deteriorate. One of the most exciting virtues of genuine love is that it can be developed within your character without the help of affectionate feelings. Before we look at genuine love, let's first consider the other two common types of love.

COMPANIONSHIP

Here, we're talking about the "I like you" feelings we have toward the opposite sex. The kind of love that pleasantly stimulates all five senses. She smells good, feels good, sounds good and looks good. She is pleasant company because she makes you feel happy. You love her like you "love pizza" or you "love country and western music".

Many relationships begin with this type of love. We all notice attractive features in others. Soon we find ourselves merging with them, enjoying the parts of our lives that make us feel good.

Though this love is the foundation for many marriages, it doesn't always withstand the pressure of time. After two or three years, the wife changes her lifestyle and hairdo while her husband opts for a new cologne and different political views. The older they get, the more they change.

We all change to some degree each year. The danger arises when we base our love on changeable characteristics we found attractive on the "companionship" level. Our feelings grow colder and colder until we finally wonder what we ever liked about our mates in the first place. So we're off to look for someone new to love. It's easy to see why "companionship love" has trouble maturing.

PASSION

Passion works harder on the emotions than companionship. It's the type of love that keeps the heart working overtime. . . "Hey, you really turn me on!" The Greeks called it eros — a sensual and physical form of love that often produces ardent physical involvement before and after marriage. Eros love heightens our senses and stimulates our bodies and minds.

GENUINE LOVE

Genuine love is completely different. It means, "I see a need in you. Let me have the privilege of meeting it." Instead of taking for itself, genuine love gives to others. It motivates us to help others reach their full potential in life.

Most importantly, genuine love has no qualifications. It doesn't say, "I'll be your friend if you'll be mine." Nor does it say, "I want you to be my girlfriend because you are beautiful and I want people to see us together," nor "I want to be your friend because your family is rich." This love does not seek to gain, but only to give. Don't you remember those junior high crushes when you said, "Well, I'll like her if she likes me, but if she gives me a bad time, I'm dumping her." Genuine love has no such "fine print".

I did a lot of research on the types of love. At the University of California at Long Beach, my biggest discovery was my life lacked genuine love. Entering a college auditorium one day, I began to look around as I normally did for friends with whom to sit. As I scanned the rows, I saw someone sitting alone and realized it was selfish of me to limit my company to those who made me feel good. I forced myself to walk over and sit next to that lone student, even though I felt awkward. That was only the beginning of my lifelong desire to develop genuine love.

THE LOWEST LEVEL OF MATURITY

The ability to love in a selfless way is dependent upon your level of maturity. The emotions listed below are typical of immature love. Check the ones characteristic of your life.

Jealousy is caused by a fear of losing something or someone we value.

Envy springs from a desire to possess what someone else has.

Anger is the inner turmoil and frustration we feel when we cannot control people or circumstances.

Loneliness results from a dependence on other people for our happiness.

Fear results when we feel scared our needs will not be met.

If you want to continue this exercise, you should make a list of the incidents that triggered each emotion you checked. Then ask yourself, "Why did I feel the emotion? Was I focusing on what I could get out of life or what I might lose in life?"

All these emotions are characteristic of immature love — a desire to use other people for personal happiness, a hunger for pleasure without regard for the cost. This same immaturity is behind the *abuse* of alcohol, drugs, and sex.

THE HIGHEST LEVEL OF MATURITY

I believe the more we help others achieve their full potential in life, the closer we are to maturity. Demonstrating a selfless desire for others to gain, builds lasting relationships. How can you go wrong when you develop a love that is primarily concerned with discovering your wife's specific needs and look for creative ways to meet them?

LEARNING TO DEVELOP A LASTING, MATURE LOVE

What do you think is the major stumbling block for most husbands in developing a lasting love for their mates? I have found that it is failing to meet a woman's needs from *her viewpoint*.

When Anna told me she felt unloved in special areas, Mike was dumbfounded. "What do you mean?" he asked her. "Well, for years you have been a great husband and a very helpful person, and you've done a lot of nice things for me," she explained gently. "But sometimes you do things I don't need. I'd appreciate it if you'd find out what is important to *me*."

A man's brilliant idea can backfire. Like the time I decided to have our house painted as a special surprise for my wife. What was special to me wasn't so special to her. Although she appreciated the paint job, she would have much rather had a new kitchen floor. When I realized that, I stopped my projects long enough to buy her a new kitchen floor. Then we made a list of priorities from her point of view. They were so different from mine!

Example after example has strengthened my belief that doing things for others "*our*" way is a selfish, immature form of love. My heart goes out to those wives who have received pool tables for Christmas, tickets to the fishing swamps of Louisiana, or invitations to the Motorman's Ball.

If you've never done so, find out what your wife needs to feel fulfilled as a woman. Then look for special ways to fulfill her needs. At first she may not believe your changes will last. Don't despair. It takes a long time to develop a sturdy relationship.

After hearing a lecture on love and marriage, one man surprised his wife with a box of candy and a dozen roses. "Oh, this is terrible," she said weeping, "The baby cut his finger real bad. Then I burned your dinner when I couldn't get rid of the vacuum cleaner salesman, the sink is stopped up. . .and now YOU come home drunk!"

Don't be surprised if your wife doesn't understand your actions at first. It took at least two years before mine would admit that I really had changed. Now she knows I am committed to spending the rest of my life sharpening my skills to meet her needs.

Learning how to love your wife in a mature way is like raising a productive vegetable garden. If you have ever tried it, you will appreciate the comparison. Our first year in Texas we decided to grow a vegetable garden. After we dug a small plot, I dumped nearly half a bag of fertilizer on it and let it sit for three months to be sure I'd have a lush garden. But something went wrong. When the carrots came up, they were a little brown around the edges. All the tomatoes began to rot on the bottom before they ripened, so we had to pick them while they were green. None of our beans survived above the half-foot level, and our cucumbers bit the dust.

I was truly puzzled until an expert gardener told me I had "burned" my vegetables with too much fertilizer. My intentions were good, but my knowledge was limited. A husband can fail in much the same way if he doesn't know exactly how much of each "love ingredient" his wife needs. In fact, this book was written to give you some very specific guidelines for "growing" a stronger marriage.

I've met many wives who looked just like my garden does now: "full of weeds and overrun with bermuda grass" because they have been neglected by their husbands. I've often thought how great it would be if vegetables could talk. If only the beans could have said, "Hey, you up there! You put way too much fertilizer in this garden and we're having a tough time. The fumes are killing us and if you don't do something about it, we're all going to die." Why if my vegetables could talk, I could have the world's greatest garden. Fortunately my wife can talk. I *can* ask her just *what* she needs, *how much* she needs, and *when* she needs it.

Wives, if you are reading this part of the book, let me assure you that we as husbands generally *do not* know what you need. Our thought processes are different; we live in a different world. So we ask you to help us learn by telling us your needs in a gentle, loving way. Let us know when we aren't meeting your needs — but not in a critical way that could cause us to lose interest.

"Many times I just want my husband to hold me in his arms and say nothing when he's hurt me," a wife told me. "But no, he'll just turn his back to me, silent and cold." I advised her that the next time he hurt her, she should tell him her needs and exactly what she desires at the time.

Since meeting your wife's needs is the golden key to a fulfilling marriage, the rest of this book deals with that subject.

Your wife's needs.

I believe a woman needs to be in harmony with her husband through a very deep intimate relationship.

She needs to sense that electric feeling when her husband walks into the room. She needs comradeship, harmony, and a feeling of togetherness.

To satisfy your wife, I believe you need to make a dedicated effort to meet each of her needs explained below:

1. Your wife needs to feel that she is first place in your life, more important than your mother, your daughter, your friends, and your secretary.
2. She needs to know that you are willing to share an intimate moment of comfort without demanding explanation or giving lectures.
3. Her need for open communication is constant. You should always maintain a clear conscience by asking forgiveness for your offenses.
4. She longs to be praised so she can feel valuable.
5. She wants to feel free to correct you without fearing retaliation and anger.
6. She needs to know that you will defend and protect her.
7. She wants to know that her opinion is so valuable that you will discuss decisions with her, evaluate her advice, and then act on it.
8. She needs to share her life with you in every area — home, family, and outside interests.
9. She wants you to be the kind of man her son can follow and her daughter would want to marry.

When her needs are met, a woman gains security and glows with a feeling of well-being. Some of her glow will rub off on you, especially if you are responsible for it in the first place.

Remember, if you try to meet her needs and blow it, Chapter Five will help you get back on the track.

THREE SAFEGUARDS IN READING THE REST OF THIS BOOK

I hope you will practice these "built-in" safeguards with each chapter you read since the ideas I put forth are general in nature. First, discuss each chapter with your wife to see where she agrees and disagrees. Think of her as a flower. All flowers are beautiful, but each needs a specific amount of sunlight, nutrients, and water to flourish. You need to meet her *unique needs* as they change from year to year.

Second, after she has shared her unique needs, rephrase them in your own words until *she* says you picked up her meaning. It is your responsibility to find out what your wife means when she says, "You said you'd be back in a *little while*." A little while might mean thirty minutes to her and two hours to you.

Third, it is important to remember how much you both differ as male and female. In general, a wife is naturally more sensitive and more aware of life than her husband. Try to understand that she will probably feel, see, and hear more than you. When your wife says something to you, allow it to sink in. Make an extra effort to understand your relationship as she sees it.

The rest of the chapter will be devoted to showing you at least one hundred ways you can "love" your wife *her way*. Ask your wife to check the ones that are meaningful to her and then arrange them in order of importance to her. Use the list to discuss each idea with her to find out her views about it. I know your relationship will be greatly strengthened as you learn how to use these suggestions:

1. Communicating with her, never closing her out. *I feel this now / feel closed out*
2. Regarding her as important. *OK*
3. Doing everything you can to understand her feelings. *need this*
4. Being interested in her friends. *OK*
5. Asking her opinion frequently. *OK*
6. Valuing what she says. *OK*
7. Letting her feel your approval and affection. *feel this now*

8. Protecting her on a daily basis. *Ok*
9. Being gentle and tender with her. *Sometimes*
10. Developing a sense of humor. *not with me*
11. Avoiding sudden major changes in her life without giving her time to adjust.
12. Learning to respond openly and verbally when she wants to communicate. *mostly listen + make sense*
13. Comforting her when she is down emotionally. For instance, putting your arms around her and silently holding her for a few seconds. *does sometimes*
14. Being interested in what she feels is important in life. *doesn't care how I feel*
15. Correcting her gently and tenderly. *doesn't do*
16. Allowing her to teach you without putting up your defenses. *doesn't do*
17. Making special time available to her and your children. *doesn't do*
18. Being trustworthy. *Ok*
19. Complimenting her often. *OK*
20. Being creative when you express your love, either in words or actions. *Don't have to be fancy - just express*
21. Having specific family goals for each year. *don't have*
22. Letting her buy things she considers necessary. *Ok*
23. Being forgiving when she offends you. *most of the time*
24. Showing her you need her. *Sometimes*
25. Accepting her the way she is. *Sometimes*
26. Admitting your mistakes. Not being afraid to be humble. *Sometimes*
27. Leading your family in their spiritual relationship with God. *Ok*
28. Allowing your wife to fail, discussing what went wrong, after you have comforted her. *OK*
29. Rubbing her feet or neck after a hard day. *doesn't do*
30. Taking time for the two of you to sit and talk calmly. *hardly ever*
31. Going on romantic outings. *don't do enough of*
32. Writing her a letter occasionally, telling her how much you love her. *doesn't do*
33. Surprising her with a card or flowers. *Sometimes*
34. Expressing how much you appreciate her. *Sometimes*
35. Telling her how proud you are of her. *OK*
36. Giving advice in a loving way when she asks for it. *need work on*
37. Defending her to others. *OK*
38. Not preferring others over her. *OK*

39. Not expecting her to do activities beyond her emotional or physical capabilities. *OK*
40. Praying for her to enjoy God's best in life. *don't know*
41. Taking time to notice what she has done for you and the family. *OK*
42. Bragging about her to other people behind her back. *don't know*
43. Sharing your thoughts and feelings with her. *Sometimes*
44. Telling her about your job if she is interested. *OK*
45. Taking time to see how she spends her day, at work or at home. *Sometimes*
46. Learning to enjoy what she enjoys. *some things*
47. Taking care of the kids before dinner. *doesn't pertain now*
48. Helping straighten up the house before meal time. *no way*
49. Letting her take a bubble bath while you do the dishes. *no way*
50. Understanding her physical limitations if you have several children. *doesn't pertain*
51. Disciplining the children in love, not anger.
52. Helping her finish her goals — hobbies or education. *OK*
53. Treating her as if God had stamped on her forehead, "Handle with care." *no way*
54. Getting rid of habits that annoy her. *doesn't do*
55. Being gentle and thoughtful to her relatives. *most of the time*
56. Not comparing her relatives with yours in a negative way. *OK*
57. Thanking her for things she has done without expecting anything in return. *OK*
58. Not expecting a band to play whenever you help with the house cleaning. *OK doesn't help much however*
59. Making sure she understands everything you are planning to do. *most of the time*
60. Doing little things for her — an unexpected kiss, coffee in bed. *hardly ever*
61. Treating her as an intellectual equal. *OK most of time*
62. Finding out if she wants to be treated as physically weaker. *What no*
63. Discovering her fears in life. *no*
64. Seeing what you can do to eliminate her fears. *no*
65. Discovering her sexual needs. *need more*
66. Asking if she wants to discuss how you can meet her sexual needs. *They are okay but more maybe*

67. Finding out what makes her insecure. *need more love,*
concern,& cuddling
68. Planning your future together. *what future? Is there a*
69. Not quarrelling over words, but trying to find hidden
meanings. *I say mean things because I feel*
neglected
70. Practicing common courtesies like holding the door for her,
pouring her coffee. *most of the time – not car*
71. Asking if you offend her sexually in any way. *does not* *doors*
72. Asking if she is jealous of anyone. *Maybe one* *other*
73. Seeing if she is uncomfortable about the way money is
spent. *No I'm not*
74. Taking her on dates now and then. *every Friday*
75. Holding her hand in public. *OK*
76. Putting your arm around her in front of friends. *OK*
77. Telling her you love her as often as you can. *Sometimes*
78. Remembering anniversaries, birthdays, and other special
occasions. *OK*
79. Learning to enjoy shopping. *does not*
80. Teaching her to hunt and fish or whatever you enjoy doing. *does not*
81. Giving her a special gift from time to time. *hardly ever*
82. Sharing the responsibilities around the house. *Not much*
83. Not belittling her feminine characteristics. *OK*
84. Letting her express herself freely, without fear of being
called stupid or illogical. *OK*
85. Carefully choosing your words, especially when angry. *not so*
86. Not criticizing her in front of others. *OK most of time*
87. Not letting her see you become excited about the physical
features of another woman if that bothers her. *OK*
88. Being sensitive to other people. *Sometimes not*
89. Letting your family know you want to spend special time
with them. *No*
90. Fixing dinner for her from time to time. *NO*
91. Being sympathetic when she is sick. *OK*
92. Calling her when you are going to be late. *OK*
93. Not disagreeing with her in front of the children. *Sometimes*
94. Taking her out to dinner and weekend-get-aways. *need more*
95. Doing the "little things" she needs from time to time. *work on*
96. Giving her special time to be alone or with her friends. *doesn't*
97. Buying her what she considers an intimate gift. *no*
like

98. Reading a book she recommends to you. *usually Takes offense* *Please read This*
99. Giving her an engraved plaque assuring her of your lasting *one* love. *No*
100. Writing her a poem about how special she is. *No*

3

If your wife doesn't win first place, you lose!

The entire airplane came to life as the popular cheerleading squad of an NFL Football team cheered in the aisle.

After they finished their enthusiastic yells, I interviewed some of the married ones. I found they faced many of the same problems other married women do. One cheerleader said her greatest disappointment was knowing she was not the most important person in her husband's life.

"Even our dog is more important to him than I am," she said. "He comes home and plays with the dog and then it's more of a, 'When's dinner going to be ready?' attitude," she sighed.

A woman's sparkling affection toward her husband is diminished when he begins to prefer other activities or people over her. Many times he is not even aware of the way his misplaced priorities damage her and their relationship. For a marriage to flourish, a wife desperately needs to know she has a very special place in her husband's heart.

Many husbands are shocked when their wives leave them "for no reason" after twenty or even thirty years of marriage. They feel they provided everything their wives could have possibly needed — a nice home, a good car, enough money to raise the children. Yet that wasn't enough, for a woman needs much more.

I have met creative businessmen who make large sums of money with their business skills, aptly keeping their employees satisfied with respect and an awareness of their needs. Isn't it ironic that such intelligent men can go home at night and not even know how to apply the same principles to their wives?

Without meaning to, a husband can communicate non-verbally that other people or activities are more important to him than his wife. Haven't you heard of golf widows? Whether it is golf or tennis, club activities or community leadership, your wife and your marital happiness will suffer if most of your time and effort is directed toward some other interest with only cold leftovers for her. A wife can feel less important just by comparing the amount of time her husband spends with her to the time he spends elsewhere. Women notice how our eyes light up and our entire personality changes as we become excited about fishing or hunting or other activities. If your wife doesn't sense that same excitement in you when you're with her, she has a gnawing sense of failure because she feels she isn't as attractive to you as are your outside activities and friends. This can be devastating to a woman's sense of personal worth.

My own wife graphically illustrated this very important concept to me during our fifth year of marriage. I arrived home for lunch to find her standing very quietly at the kitchen sink, not even interested in talking when I tried to make conversation. In a moment of insight, I quickly perceived that I was in hot water. I remember her coolness toward me during the previous few days which I had mistakenly attributed to some sort of hormonal change.

"Is there anything wrong between us?" I asked her.

"It doesn't matter. You wouldn't understand anyway," she answered.

"Funny thing, I'm losing my desire to go back to work right now. I can see there are some real problems. Wouldn't you like to talk about it? I'm not sure what I'm doing wrong."

"Even if I told you, either you wouldn't understand or you wouldn't change, so what's the use? Let's don't talk about it. It hurts me. It discourages me and disappoints me when you say you're going to do something and then you don't."

But I gently persisted, telling her that I wished she would share it with me, that I just didn't understand. Finally, she was able to verbalize what actions during the past five years had driven an impenetrable wedge between us.

"You'd really rather be at work, or with your friends, or counseling people than spending time with me," she said.

I asked her to explain.

"If someone calls you when we have plans, you're liable to say 'Let me check with my wife and see if I can't postpone our plans.' I just can't believe you would do that to me over and over again."

I explained how it was easier for me to turn her down than to say no to other people.

"What about when I cook a special dinner, sometimes even with candlelight? You'll come home or call and say you've had to make other plans. You go off somewhere with other people as if I didn't even exist, as if it didn't even mean anything that I've gone to extra-special effort for you."

She continued, "I don't care anymore. I don't even want to do these special things for you. I've been disappointed so many times that I just can't handle it emotionally."

She made me realize that although I always had time for someone in need of counseling, I made no effort to spend time with her. When I did spend time with her, she said, I didn't have the same concentration or excitement about being with her.

I listened to her reveal her innermost feelings for several hours. I really didn't know what to do and I wasn't sure I'd be able to change. But I could understand her complaints. I had neglected her and offended her with my unloving ways. However, when I agreed with her, she was unresponsive and I could tell she had given up.

"Could you find it in your heart to forgive me for the way I've treated you?" I asked. "I'm willing to change. I'll really plan on changing."

"Sure, I've heard that song before," she said skeptically.

I didn't know how long it would take for me to reform, to begin to show a preference for my wife. I knew the next time someone called right before dinner I would have to ask, "Is this an emergency, or can we work it out tomorrow?" I had to show her I really meant business about meeting her needs *first*, before those of my friends.

I *wanted* to tell her she was the most important person in my life. I really *wanted* to feel that way. At first I didn't have that feeling, but I wanted to have it. As I tried to make her more important to me than anyone else, I soon *felt* she was top priority. Not only in marriage, but in so many areas of life, our feelings *follow* our thoughts and actions. In other words, the warm inner feeling I have for Norma began to burn after I placed the "Queen's crown" upon her head.

My pride was broken, my ego bruised and my feelings wounded in numerous falls from marital harmony during the first two years of living these principles. Because I tried so hard to make it work, Norma finally believed I was earnest in my endeavor to change. But it took two years to convince her.

I learned from Norma and other wives that women need to see effort and not hear mere promises. Give your wife time to watch you climb the mountain if she doesn't believe what you say initially. Show her you are learning to scale the cliffs and hurdle the crevices. The more *consistently* loving we are as husbands, the more trustworthy we become to our wives. Soon they will join us as we climb hand over hand toward the goal of a loving marriage.

THE EVIDENCE WIVES NEED BEFORE THEY WILL BELIEVE THEIR HUSBANDS

Wives need proof of change in at *least three areas* before they will believe their husbands' commitment.

1. CAREFUL LISTENING WITHOUT JUSTIFICATION OR ARGUMENT

Can you imagine a husband being able to justify everything he ever did to hurt his wife? Wayne thought he could. He and his wife couldn't talk for more than fifteen minutes before falling into a heated argument. Inevitably, through his logical deductions, the argument ended up being her fault.

Finally, Wayne told Cathy he really wanted to learn, to change and to love her. A few hours later she suggested a quiet little vacation, just for the two of them to get reacquainted. "Couldn't we just take a week's vacation?" she asked.

"Are you kidding?" he replied, crushing her hopes for better understanding. "You mean you want me to pay rent here at the apartment and then pay for a motel too? That's double rent!"

The topic developed into a fight that led to more fights as the months went by, until their relationship deteriorated and she finally left. He had refused to listen to her needs without arguing and lost her as a result.

It is often difficult for a man to converse with his wife without challenging the meaning of various words she uses to explain how she feels inside. If a husband can *overlook the actual word* his wife uses to express herself and instead actively pursue *what she means*, far less arguments will take place. One man I know finds it almost impossible to do this. When his wife uses phrases like "you *never* do this," or "you *always* do that," he will inevitably say, "Now, dear, I don't *always* do that." Or he begins to analyze her statement to prove its fallacy. In ten minutes, they're off on another hot discussion. It is essential in communication to *look past the words* to the real meaning.

There is no meaning in a word. Meaning is in people.
Everyone has his own definition for a given word. We attach meanings to words based on our own unique experiences. So when we attempt to communicate with another person, we use words we believe will accurately convey our thoughts. For instance, in this book I may use words that you enjoy, or words that turn you off or irritate you. You might even be indifferent to my words because you have a different frame of reference. Since my definitions might be different than yours, I try to illustrate all the important points I make, probing for our common point of reference.

You can do the same with your wife. If you can stop justifying your actions and quit arguing about the words your wife uses, you can get down to the heart of the matter. Try rephrasing your wife's statements until she says you have grasped her meaning. "Is this what you're saying, Dear?" or "Is this what I'm hearing?" At all cost, avoid sarcastic questions like, "Is this what you're having trouble saying. . ?" A budding relationship between husband and wife can be stunted by an attitude of male superiority.

2. QUICKNESS TO ADMIT HIS ERROR

Countless wives and children have told me how their family

relationships were weakened because of a husband's or father's unwillingness to admit his errors. Though husbands sometimes think admission of error reveals their weaknesses, the opposite is true. Just think back through your own life to the times when someone admitted his offense to you. Chances are, your respect for him or her increased, not decreased.

A probation officer who is a personal friend of mine made a racially derogatory statement to an associate during the day. His friend was offended; however, the situation was not discussed. The probation officer drove away feeling somewhat uneasy and guilty for what he had said. Before he reached his home, he turned around and drove back to confront the man.

Walking into the room, he said, "A few moments ago, I said something very offensive to you. I know it was wrong and I have come back to ask if you could forgive me for what I said."

The man nearly fell over. Of course he forgave him, and his respect for the officer doubled. I can't think of an exception to the rule that a humble admission of wrong produces positive results. When a husband admits he has hurt his wife, she feels better just knowing he understands. His admission of wrong produces a much stronger marriage.

3. PATIENCE WHEN SHE IS RELUCTANT TO BELIEVE HE'S CHANGED

What if you've been doing everything within your power to let her know she's first place in your life, and she still doesn't believe you've changed? Do you throw up your arms in disgust or gently persuade her over a period of time? I hope you choose the latter. Her initial respect for you wasn't lost overnight, and it can't be regained in a day. Show her that no matter how long it takes, you want to earn her respect.

What causes a man to come home after work, pick up his young son, and kiss and cuddle him without even greeting his wife? How can a husband walk straight to the garage to begin a project without even acknowledging his arrival to his wife as he passes by her in the kitchen? I think two important factors may explain *why* a man *loses* a degree of affection and enthusiasm for his wife after marriage.

TWO REASONS WHY A WIFE CAN BECOME LESS IMPORTANT TO HER HUSBAND

1. A man will pursue and charm a woman with words, or flowers or whatever he needs to do to *win* her. But after the wedding, he feels he has conquered her. She is his, so he doesn't have to maintain the same level of enthusiasm and creativity as he did before they married. She is his emotionally and legally. The husband may say to himself, "I have my wife. Now, I need to conquer my business or I need to become a better hunter or we need to begin a family." Each frontier is viewed as a new conquest, a new experience.

2. Almost anything is sweet to a starving man, but when he's full, even honey nauseates him. In a very real sense, a man is filled up when he marries because his wife is now a part of him. He has experienced knowing her in every way — spiritually, emotionally, mentally and physically. He may feel there is nothing left to know about her. He is satisfied and therefore, has a natural tendency to look for other potential "frontiers" almost immediately following marriage.

I believe it is healthy for a husband and wife to put a creative sparkle into their relationship by remaining a challenge to each other. I remember this was the motivating factor in my attraction to Norma. We had been dating casually for three years when I heard she had fallen in love with someone else. At the moment I visualized losing her, I became far more creative, challenging myself to restore our relationship. But like so many other men, after we married I focused upon other conquests such as school and my career. Since it was no longer a priority to earn her affection, I simply went on to oil whatever wheel squeaked the loudest. Now, I find when a wife can learn to put a little mystique back into the relationship, it tantalizes her husband. That mystique is not simply "playing hard to get"; it is more a matter of being secure in herself. It's letting her husband know she is not totally dependent upon him.

HOW TO GAIN YOUR WIFE'S LOVE AND MORE

If it came down to an evening with your friends or a night with your wife, she needs to know you would choose her company just because you enjoy being with her. In the same way, if it came to the children or her, she needs to know she would be your choice. She needs to know she's Number One. When she is satisfied that she's in first place in your life, she will encourage you to do the other things you like doing. For example, I am taking six weeks away from my wife and children to write this book. Several years ago my wife would have been crushed by a mere suggestion of such a long separation. Yet, today she is as enthusiastic about it as I am because she knows I will be able to fulfill *our* life-long dream of sharing our inner convictions about marriage. More importantly, she knows I would rather be with her than with my typewriter and editor.

Putting your wife in the Number One slot doesn't shackle you to the house; instead, it frees you of the dread of going home.

"Why don't you let me go to the meeting alone tonight so you can go to the basketball game?" Mary said. Her husband was pleasantly shocked. Not so long ago they had misunderstandings about his unsatiable appetite for basketball. Just a short while back this couple was thinking about separating because the husband did not have the knowledge or skills he needed to treat her right and she did not have the emotional strength to continue living with him or loving him. Today he regularly puts her before his work, his activities, etc. And she is now free to encourage his outside interests, knowing she's at the top of his list.

My wife also encourages me to enjoy my interests in hunting and fishing as long as she feels secure in her position of importance. If an emergency arose, she knows I would be much more committed to taking care of her than I would be to finishing my recreational enjoyment.

> THE MORE IMPORTANT A WOMAN FEELS SHE IS TO HER HUSBAND, THE MORE SHE ENCOURAGES HIM TO DO THE ACTIVITIES SHE KNOWS HE ENJOYS — ACTIVITIES SHE USED TO RESENT.

Do you wonder if your wife feels more important to you than other people or things in your life? I'd like for you to complete the following project to find out. First list your favorite spare time activities.

_____

_____

_____

_____

_____

What is an enjoyable "after work" activity for you?

Monday _____

Tuesday _____

Wednesday _____

Thursday _____

Friday _____

Saturday _____

Sunday _____

Where do you enjoy taking your vacations?

_____

_____

_____

Look back over those three lists and ask yourself, "*Is there anything on the lists I would rather do than be with my wife?*" Probably so. I would be surprised if you couldn't name a few activities you enjoy more than your wife's company. Chances are, you have already "communicated" to your wife that she is not as important to you as those activities even though you have never uttered those words. Since a woman has tremendous perception, you don't have to say anything for her to know where your heart is. . .But that doesn't mean it's too late to change.

YOUR WIFE'S "RADAR" CAN DETECT YOUR SINCERITY

What a man values, he takes good care of. If your hobby is

fishing, you probably hesitate to loan out your rod and reel. If you enjoy hunting, you probably know how to carefully oil and polish guns. Based on the amount of time you spend on each activity, your wife can sense which is most important to you. If she doesn't feel that you are as careful with her as you are with your other interests, she will know she is not as important. That feeling shatters her self-worth and can result in physical as well as emotional problems. The emotions she struggles with now may surface years later in the form of serious and expensive physical problems.

When a woman is aware that her husband is treating her in a special way, their relationship grows deeper and becomes more lasting. However, some husbands feel threatened by the thought of giving their wives special treatment, fearing they will lose out with their friends, career or hobbies. They falsely believe if they give up other activities for the sake of being with their wives, they will give them up forever. Remember, when a wife feels she is the most important, she gets excited about her husband being able to do the things he wants to do.

HOW I GAINED MY WIFE'S LOVE
AND EVERYTHING ELSE

After ten years of marriage, I felt I was finally becoming a success at my work. I was privileged to speak for various organizations in our city and throughout the country. My wife and I had a beautiful home and two children. What more could a man want? Then from my point of view, a tragedy occurred in my marriage. Norma became pregnant with our third child. I was not enthusiastic. If anything, I was depressed, realizing our youngest had only been out of diapers for three years. I was just now starting to enjoy my children, and the thought of another little baby around the house was almost overwhelming.

Although I tried to be nice to Norma, I couldn't hide my disappointment. I was afraid I might not be able to travel as much or that I would be forced to take a position in the company with less prestige. My work load increased as the months passed, and I warned my wife I would not be able to help her with the children because of job demands. Even on the day my son was born, I worried about the added hardships he would add to my vocational dreams.

Norma's health suffered during the first year after our son's birth because of the long night hours and the responsibility of taking care of two other small children. Our baby had to have surgery and was often sick, adding to her burden. I can remember how cruel I was during that year. Whenever he would cry at night or need special attention, I would quickly remind Norma he was her child. She had wanted another baby, I hadn't.

A year passed this way before finally Norma came to me and said, "I can't take it anymore. I wish I had the emotional and physical strength to take care of the kids, discipline and train them, but I just can't do it with an absentee father."

She wasn't demanding. She wasn't angry. She simply stated the facts. She had had it. I could see the urgency in her facial expressions and realized that she desperately needed my help. I faced a major decision. Should I go to my boss and ask for a different job in the company? Ask for a job that would allow me more time at home? It was a struggle because I knew I would get a less prestigious job. I felt I would have to sacrifice some of my career goals. Inwardly, I felt resentment toward my son and my wife for being weak. But, I gave in. In nervousness and embarrassment, I approached my boss to explain I needed more time at home because of the children. "Is there any possibility that I could have a different job that would allow me to stay home more?"

My boss graciously cooperated by giving me another job. But to me the new job was a demotion. I was asked to do some things only a few weeks earlier I had been training my subordinates to do. What a blow!

I was devastated for awhile, but soon I became interested in home life. I actually looked forward to five o'clock though I used to ignore it. My family and I began doing more things together, like camping and other special activities. Before long, a new love blossomed within both of us. Norma began to feel more physically alert which, in turn, made her more cheerful and outgoing. She changed some habits I disliked without any pressure from me. My "big" career sacrifice seemed smaller every day.

Within a few months, my boss gave me a new position in the company that I liked best of all. By this time, Norma was so secure with me that she had no resentment of my new job and travel. I gave in and gave up at first, but I won in the long run.

THE INCREDIBLE RESULTS OF
MAKING YOUR WIFE FEEL IMPORTANT

One morning Sandy was so sexually responsive to Rick that he was stunned and surprised by her excitement. How did Rick motivate her? One very simple statement. He was getting ready for work that morning, running a little late when he heard Sandy complaining of a growing headache and neckache.

"Let me rub your neck," he offered.

"No, you don't have time," she replied. "You've got to get to work."

His usual response would have been, "Yeah, you're right. I don't want to be late, but I hope you feel better. Take an aspirin."

On this particular morning he said, "I tell you what. I'd rather be with you, let me rub your neck." As he gently massaged her tense muscles, he continued, "*Work can wait. . .You're more important to me than that.*" She was so thrilled with his attitude and so encouraged by his sensitivity and gentleness, she said she could hardly resist giving herself to him in every way.

We men are not aware of the effects we have on our wives by being gentle and tender, showing our unshakeable devotion.

Do you want a more enjoyable marriage? It's possible. I believe it all starts by loving your wife more than anyone or any activity.

Here are a few questions you can ask your wife, to open up a discussion concerning her real feelings about the place she shares in your life:

1. Do you feel like you are the most important person in my life? *I Don't Know*
2. Are there any activities in my life you feel are more important to me than you are? *Yes*
3. Are there any special ways you believe I could better communicate how important you are to me? *Wanting To be with me more Than (doing anything else.)*

Remember, the more you do to build a healthy relationship, the better you'll feel about your marriage. If you change any of your activities because you want to enrich your relationship, at first you may feel you're giving up your favorite pastime. But in the long run, you'll not only gain a better marriage, but a greater freedom to enjoy life. Today I wouldn't trade my deep friendship with Norma for anything on this earth. I am finding that the more important a man's wife is to him, the more she encourages him to enjoy himself.

My husband feels I'm asking Too much of him when I say I want To be with him more. He doesn't want To set around + cudelle and Love because he Thinks That is not important any more. He Thinks it is stupid and not necessary (we are not newly weds in other words) or he Thinks I'm being Too possesive of his Time. Mean while our marriage is going down The drain. He would rather give up, Than change.

4

She needs your shoulder,
not your mouth

As I pulled into the driveway, I heard a sickening thump under the tire. Only a few seconds earlier our cat had been running happily toward our car to welcome us home.

"Watch out for Puff," Norma said.

"Oh, he'll get out of the way," I replied.

I hadn't been driving fast. "How fast can you pull into a driveway?" I thought.

"Oh, no!" I whispered, "Can someone get me out of this mess?" My family thought it was just another one of my jokes about wanting to get rid of our two cats.

My oldest son jumped out of the car to run in for a flashlight. When he looked underneath the car, he fell to the ground screaming. My daughter Kari was sobbing and my youngest son woke up from his nap to join the chorus. Bedlam set in. They all started accusing me of purposely killing the cat. How I regretted the times I had joked about it.

Puff was the kitten of our other cat. We all loved the mother cat, but we loved Puff much more. He was the only kitten of the litter we had kept because of his "puffy" hernia. His stomach grew larger and larger until finally I had to give in and take him to a veterinarian to have the hernia repaired. But the operation was a failure. A few months later, I had to take him back for another operation. And I didn't even want the cat in the first place. I told my family, "This cat sure is costing me a lot." I was saying things men typically say, blind to the hurt I was causing my family.

Now that I had run over the cat, I was under attack. When they started screaming at me, I wanted to yell back. But the things Norma had shared with me in the past about herself, our children, and women in general strangled the words. "Don't talk, just hold me or hold the kids whenever there's a tragedy," she had said.

They were making so much racket in the front yard, I knew the neighbors were going to think I was killing them. I was so embarrassed and crushed that I herded them all into the house. I put my arm around Kari and hugged her. But as I hugged Greg, I could tell he didn't want me to touch him. I tried to put my arm around Norma, but she gave me one of those familiar looks a woman saves for times when her husband bombs out.

"This is what you always wanted, isn't it?" she asked. "You wanted him dead." With that, she marched into the bedroom and closed the door.

But I still didn't say anything. I didn't get angry, though I felt my family misunderstood me. I knew that raising my voice wouldn't help. Since Michael didn't want me to touch him either, Greg and I went out to the driveway to get Puff and bury him. We took him to our little burial ground where Peter, our rabbit rests. Greg was still sobbing, "Dad, life will never be the same." Greg loved that cat just about as much as you can love anything. As Greg and I buried him, I prayed and Greg concluded the funeral service.

My stomach was nauseated when I went back inside. There stood my twelve-year-old, Kari, comforting Michael, our five-year-old. "Michael, it was Puff's time to go. It was Puff's time."

When Greg was getting ready for bed, I went to his room and held him. His eyes red, he asked, "Dad, what am I going to do when I come home from school? What am I going to do, Dad? Puff won't be there to jump into my arms.'' And I cried too.

Courageous little Kari was standing in the hall after putting Michael to bed. "Well Dad, it's all over," she said. "It was Puff's time. I tell you what Dad, I think we can eat those donuts now." We had bought donuts and milk right before we came home, planning a quiet family snack.

"Kari, you can if you want, but I just wouldn't be able to eat. I just can't eat tonight," I told her.

Opening the door to our bedroom, I wondered if my wife was ready to face me yet. She had told me many times in the past, "Don't demand anything. Wait until I am able to respond to you." Don't Push yourself on me.

I got down on my knees next to her, gently touching her hand and asked, "How are you feeling?"

"I'm feeling better. I know you didn't mean to do it. I just couldn't handle it," she said.

"That's okay," I assured her. "I understand. You know all those things I said when I was joking about Puff? I really feel bad about them. You can rest assured I'll never joke about things like that again. Would it make you feel better if we made Angel an 'inside' cat from now on?"

From time to time, I say to Norma, "You know, I really do feel bad that you don't have Puff around to jump up into your arms. " She puts her head down on my shoulder and says, "Yeah, I know, I feel bad too." Through that painful experience, I learned more about comforting my wife than I could have in years of trouble-free existence.

Let your wife teach you the same thing, showing how you can best meet her needs during a crisis.

Probably the most important lesson my wife taught me on how to comfort her was when she told me in a calm way she could not handle my busy work schedule with the pressures of the children and the home. By coming to me without threats to explain her limitations, she touched something within me. I was eager to comfort her. I don't know if she stirred my protective manly feelings or what. But when she told me she couldn't take the pressure I was putting on her and that she might be close to a collapse, I was motivated to relieve her of that pressure.

I have found that this non-threatening approach works even in a father-daughter relationship. A graduate student in a university came to me because of a poor relationship with her father. I tried to work with her father, explaining what I had learned about women. "Comfort her," I suggested. "Be tender and gentle, don't lecture her." But he couldn't grasp it. A very skilled and intelligent lawyer, he is quite successful in his profession. I have noticed that my lawyer friends have a difficult time being tender and loving without lecturing. It's drilled into them to express how they feel in a logical way. But women don't respond to lectures. They need comfort, many times with no words at all!

"I tried to take my life last week," this graduate student told me. "I just cannot handle the emotional pressure I'm under with my father."

"You've got one of two choices," I said.

"What?"

"You can respond to your father in a way that you and I know will bring healing to your life."

"I'm not able to do that," she said wearily.

"Okay, then you have another option. You have to call your father and say to him 'Daddy, I love you. I wish that I could spend more time with you but, Daddy, I feel like I just can't handle seeing you right now. I can't emotionally handle the way you treat me — your lectures, your insensitivity and your harshness. As much as I wish I could, as much as I wish I was stronger, I just can't handle it!"

This girl has unique needs and qualities. Nobody could tell her she needed to be stronger. She is who she is. To tell her to be what she can't be is like saying to the sun, "Don't come up tomorrow." It's reality!

Happily, her Dad was motivated to change, thinking, "I must really be insensitive. My own daughter can't handle my presence. She can't even handle a phone call from me."

Financially, he had been very generous to her, but she needed his love and gentleness much more than she needed his money. A man doesn't realize tender love is all a woman needs at times. Just a comforting hug, a loving statement like, "I understand. You're hurting aren't you? You are feeling under a lot of pressure, aren't you?"

GIVE HER YOUR SHOULDER, NOT YOUR MOUTH!

Your goal should be to become a gentle, loving and tender husband who does not lecture. Lectures during stressful times only create more stress. This was a new concept to me because I wasn't lucky enough to have a father who knew how to be tender to his wife. I wasn't aware of a woman's need for tenderness until a few years ago. No one ever told me that's what a woman needs, and even if they had I don't think I would have understood. I should have been able to figure it out, though, because even when I am down, I like for people to be gentle and comforting to me.

I'll never forget what a woman told me, "If my husband would only put his arm around me and hold me without lecturing me when I am feeling blue." But lecture #734 would begin as he told her she would feel better if she took an aspirin, if she were more organized, if she wouldn't wear herself down so much, if she would discipline the children better. . .That is not what a woman needs!

"Have you ever told him what you need?" I asked.

"Are you kidding? I'd be embarrassed," she laughed. "Come on, you're kidding."

"No, he probably doesn't know what to do. He doesn't know you need to be held instead of lectured. Why don't you tell him during a calm conversation some day?"

"That does kind of make sense to me. A lot of times when I am down and crying and all upset, he'll ask 'What do you want me to do?' I just flare up and say, 'If I have to tell you what to do, it would wreck the whole idea.' "

As a husband, I recommend that you ask your wife what her needs are. You've got to find out somewhere. You may find it in a book, have it revealed by God in a special way, be told by another woman, or see it practiced by another man. You can't dream it up on your own. We men just can't perceive the deep feelings of our wives. We've got to draw them out and then practice, practice, practice the skills of meeting their needs.

The first time I ever tried to ski, I rode a rope pulley to the top of a small hill. The hill looked a lot bigger from the top than it did from the bottom.

I thought, "No way am I gonna go down this hill." So I laid on my back and scooted all the way down.

Even if you have to scoot instead of ski your way through the skills in this chapter at first, remember that you'll eventually get the hang of it. This book is certainly not an exhaustive marriage manual, but it is a start. Believe me, if you practice what is written here, you and your wife can have a more loving marriage.

When I was first learning the art of comforting my wife, we had an experience that took every ounce of self-control I could muster. But I came through a stronger man, encouraged by my new found strength. I want you to imagine yourself in my situation to see how you would have reacted.

I had bought a dumpy looking boat for $400 because we wanted to do more things together as a family. That same night my son and I decided to take it for a quick trip to the lake only five minutes from our house just to see how it ran. Because of my inexperience as a boater, the wind blew it back to the bank the first time I put it in. I got wet and frustrated trying to push it out again. After an irritating ten minutes trying to start the cantankerous thing, the boat wouldn't go faster than ten miles an hour. Something was obviously wrong. I was quite a way from the shore before realizing I had better get back in case the motor stalled.

"Dad, the boat's sinking!" Greg cried. I looked behind me and saw the foot of water that had gurgled in. The previous owner had taken the plug out the last time it had rained. He hadn't remembered to tell me, though. With the hull full of water, I couldn't find the hole for the plug. Luckily we didn't sink. I put the boat back on the trailer, determined to take it back first thing in the morning. I was a little embarrassed to have the dumpy looking thing parked in front of my house anyway.

A boat dealer told me it would take $150 to fix the engine's broken seal, so I returned it to the owner who had promised me I could have my money back if I didn't like it.

When I left home early that morning I agreed to be back by 11 o'clock so my wife could go shopping. Retrieving my money took longer than I had planned, and I arrived home an hour and a half late. In the meantime, she had decided to take our mini-motor home to the grocery store. Trying to turn it around in the driveway, she forgot that the cab is much narrower than the width of the home itself and she sheared-off a whole section of our roof. As the roof fell, it put a huge dent in the side of the motor home.

When I pulled into the driveway at 12:30, part of the roof was lying in the driveway next to my dented motor home. I just laughed out loud, more out of desperation than humor.

I wanted to say to my wife, "Oh, no, five-hundred dollars at least to fix this. Where did you get your driver's license, Sears and Roebuck?" I wanted to lecture her angrily and then ignore her for a while.

For once, I remembered what I was supposed to do. I told myself, "Keep your mouth shut and put your arms around your wife. Just hold her. Don't say anything, okay?"

However, my basic manly nature told me, "Give her a lecture. Let your anger out. Express it."

My memory finally triumphed over my will, so I put my arms around her and said gently, "You must feel terrible, don't you?" A war was still raging inside me, but we went into the house to sit on the couch. I let her talk it out, about how badly she felt. (Most times, wives already know what they should have done. They usually know they are wrong, so a lecture is just a waste of time anyway.)

I held her, and after a couple of minutes I felt good because I could feel the tenderness begin to flow from me. Soon I was fine and she was fine. Minutes later, a carpenter who is a friend of mine drove up and we had the roof patched and painted in two hours.

It felt good not to be angry for once. I hadn't offended my wife, shouted at the kids, or diminished any of the beauty of our relationship. I could have reverted to my old cop out, "Well, I just can't keep from blowing up." But instead, I had one of those rare victories.

My new found sensitivity has been tested on several occasions. Once I almost blew it on a fishing trip. I normally become completely oblivious to my family and the world when I'm near a stream, totally "submerging" myself in the exhilarating environment of fishing: the smell of the air, the tension when a fish strikes, the sound of the stream. . .Oops! Back to the story.

When we pulled up in our mini-home to a beautiful stream, my heart was pounding and I could hardly wait to get my reel rigged up. First, I rigged the kids' reels and told them, "Look, if you get tangled up, you're on your own." I used to get so frustrated when I was trying to fish and they were yelling, "Dad, I can't get this reeled in.'' I wanted to devote my entire energy to fishing on my own.

I found the perfect spot: a nice deep hole in a pool in front of a big boulder. I threw in the lure and let it wander naturally to the bottom of the pool. It swirled around and WHAM! I got my first trout! After I nearly caught the limit, Greg came running up. I was sure he was about to jump into the stream and spook the fish. I was already upset and angry from his interruption when he said, "Dad! Kari broke her leg!"

Kari broke her leg? What a time to break her leg! I couldn't believe she would do this to me. It was hard for me to leave, but I gave the line to Greg and said, "Don't break it. Don't get it tangled up. Just keep it in there." I ran in Kari's direction avoiding the big pool. After all, I didn't want to scare the fish. Downstream Kari was crying.

"Daddy, I think I broke my leg."

When I looked at it, I realized it was only bruised.

"Don't touch it," I said. "It's not broken, it's just bruised. Put your leg in this cold water to soak for a few minutes."

I'm really embarrassed to tell the rest of the story, but maybe you can learn from my insensitivity. I ran back to the fishing hole and caught a few more trout before walking back to where Kari was crying. "Dad, this water is cold."

I rather roughly got her up to walk, but she couldn't. When I tried to hoist her up on the bank and couldn't, she started crying again and said, "Dad, you're so rough with me. Can't you be *tender*?" Something flashed when she said that word. It reminded me of all the times my wife and other women have told me, "What we need is tenderness and gentleness, not harshness. We don't need lectures." And I couldn't even be tender with my eleven-year-old daughter. I had already lectured Kari because I felt she was interrupting my day. "Why didn't you look first?" I had asked her.

Just who was more important anyway? Those trout or my precious daughter? It was hard for me to face, but those trout had been more important to me. I had let fishing and my own desires endanger my only daughter. I should have known better!

When I came to my senses, I hung my head low and said,

"Kari, I've been so wrong to be harsh with you. I really feel bad. Would you forgive me?"

"Yeah, I'll forgive you, Dad."

"Kari, you are more important to me than any fish, and I want you to know that. I was so carried away by this activity today that I really hurt you, didn't I?"

We just held each other for awhile, and then she looked up into my eyes and asked gently, "Dad, did you use deodorant today?"

HOW TO COMFORT YOUR WIFE
WHEN SHE'S DISCOURAGED

Both men and women experience stress daily. Some days are worse than others, like when I ran over Puff. Psychologists tell us that stressful experiences affect our mind, our emotions, and our body. The amount of stress we experience in each of these areas can mean the difference between happiness or depression. Positive input in any *one* area has been proven to have beneficial effects on all the other areas. If a husband is tender with his wife, for example, he lifts her emotions and, in turn, helps her in the other dimensions of her life.

According to Dr. Jerry Day, a clinical Psychologist from Tuscon, Arizona, if a wife has at least four of the following symptoms she could be diagnosed as depressed. As a husband, you need to know these signs to be able to comfort her more effectively. The list below shows symptoms you should look for in your wife:

General Symptoms of Depression

1. Sadness
2. Hopelessness

3. Loss of humor
4. Premature awakening

5. Early morning awakening

6. Insomnia
7. Feeling better as the day wears on

8. Loss of sexual interest
9. Loss of appetite and weight
10. Vague physical complaints

11. Sense of personal loss
(death of a close relative,
loss of job, etc.)

12. Poor concentration
and memory

13. Deep sighing or moaning

Should you detect these symptoms in your wife, you should comfort her first with statements like, "I sure do understand how you feel." Don't use the information below as a basis for lectures. Let it be a guideline to *help her* out of depression.

HELPING YOUR WIFE OVERCOME DEPRESSION

1. If your wife has at least four of the above symptoms, encourage her to have a complete physical examination. Her symptoms might be caused from a hormone or vitamin deficiency, or a physical illness.

2. Avoid lecturing her. Reasoning with her only makes her feel you don't understand. But sending her a card or flowers can lift her emotionally. Help your children do something special for her. For example, you can go down to the store and buy a small roll of shelf paper. Roll it out and paste on it magazine pictures that depict things you appreciate about her. With brightly colored pens, write affectionate words all over the banner. Roll it up with a pretty bow and present it to her as a family. Your thoughtful gesture will affect her emotions and *help* lift her out of the darkness.

3. Listen to your wife with the "third ear." In other words listen for her emotional message. What is she trying to say? Can you understand the meaning behind her words? Try saying something like, "I don't know why this terrible thing has happened to you, but I can really see that it has deeply upset you." By saying those words you will allow her time to gain physical strength through your understanding.

4. Help her feel better by "blocking" her symptoms. Dr. Day explained this concept to me as follows: Whenever an actor is on

stage, he has to overdo it and exaggerate to communicate a thought to the audience. Though he feels he is exaggerating, the audience perceives his behavior as normal. Dr. Day believes it is important for you to exaggerate your wife's problem so she will really believe you understand how badly she feels. She will receive your statements as normal, though you may feel you have overdone it.

For example, suggest a very hard project for her. It can be something physically exhausting like jogging, or something else that requires fierce mental effort. Tell her, "Maybe you ought to do something serious to get over this." Many times this shocks a depressed person into reality. They come away feeling, "Things aren't that bad."

When things seem hopeless, though, a depressed person often feels like sleeping the day away. Nothing could be worse. Help your wife get up and go out, even if you have to go shopping with her. My wife sometimes feels like hiding under the blanket when she's been depressed, even though she knows she will feel better if she gets up and goes to an exercise class or becomes vigorously involved in an activity.

5. Another helpful therapy for depression is writing down our thoughts. A certain "washing of the soul" occurs when we record our thoughts while in depression, Dr. Day says. Buy your wife a spiral notebook and encourage her to write down the ways you or others have hurt her.

Better yet, encourage her to write down the benefits that will enter her life as a result of the depressing things that have happened to her. She may resist at first, saying she can't think of a single benefit. You may need to come up with at least one benefit for her before she can get started. The more benefits she uncovers, the better she will feel. Most women who do this exercise end up telling me, "Things really aren't so bad."

Even when your wife can't take time to write down her feelings, you can help her avoid negative thinking. Gently steer her away from the two words "If only." Those words, one psychiatrist said, have kept more people in depression than any others. "If only I hadn't. . .if only I would. . .if only he had. . ." These two words can tear up a person emotionally, mentally, and physically.

6. Encourage your wife during stressful times to relax her muscles. An exercise by Dr. Day, that I practice regularly, can renew creativity and strength. I can personally testify that this ten-minute relaxing technique has, at times, made me feel like I've just had four hours of deep sleep. Dr. Day is currently writing a book on the subject. In a nut shell, it allows your body's natural relaxing mechanism to work: relax in a chair or on a bed, take several deep breaths, tighten every muscle in your body for as long as you can hold one deep breath, and then exhale. Visualize your muscles relaxing and then don't move a muscle for the remainder of the ten minutes.

7.   Gain a firm commitment from your wife to begin and continue a vigorous physical exercise program. We decided Norma should join a women's health club just to have a place to exercise when she feels discouraged. Physical exercise helps a person mentally and emotionally. Those who work with depressed people say it is one of the most important areas of therapy.

HOW DOES YOUR WIFE NEED TO BE COMFORTED?

Why not ask her to help you understand how and when she needs comfort? Encourage her to be patient with you until you master the skill of tenderly comforting her.

I need to be held & not lectured when something goes wrong.

5

Climbing out of marriage's deepest pit

It was 4 p.m. on Valentine's Day when I remembered my basketball game. I reached for the phone to call Norma, my bride of less than a year.

"Honey, I forgot to tell you I have a basketball game tonight. We're supposed to be there about seven o'clock. I'll pick you up about 6:30."

Silence hung heavily on the line before she answered, "But this is Valentine's Day."

"Yeah, I know, but I need to be there tonight because I promised the team. I don't want to let them down."

"But I have a special dinner prepared with candles and. . ."

"Can you hold it off until tomorrow?" She didn't answer, so I continued. "Honey, you know how important it is for a wife to submit to her husband." Little did I know that one of the worst things a husband can do is to demand submission from his wife. "I really need to be there tonight, and if we're going to start off with good habits in the early part of our marriage, now is the time to begin. If I'm going to be the leader of this family, I need to make the decision."

"Ice" perfectly described the reception I received when I picked her up. It was easy to see I had severely offended her. But I figured she had to learn to be submissive sometime, and we might as well start now. The lifeless expression on her face grew worse as the evening wore on.

When we returned home after the game, I noticed two candles on the table nicely placed beside our best dishes and pretty napkins. She still wasn't speaking to me the next day, so I rushed to the florist's to gather a variety of flowers which I put in various spots all over the house. That warmed her up a little. I gave her a giant card with a hand on the front that could be turned thumbs up or thumbs down. "Which way is it?" I asked her. She turned it thumbs up. I never said whether I was right or wrong, only that I felt badly about the night before. And so began a history of offenses I never cleared up with her.

Had someone not shared with me a year later the secret of developing a lasting and intimate relationship, we might have joined the millions who seek divorce each year. *End every day with a clean slate — no offenses between the two of you.*

Couples often ask me, "Where have we gone wrong?" "Why don't we feel romantic toward each other?" "How come we argue so much?" "Why do we avoid touching each other. . ?" These problems are not primarily attributable to incompatibility, sexual problems, financial pressure, or any other surface issues. They are a direct result of *accumulated offenses*. If a husband and wife can understand how to maintain harmony by immediately clearing up every hurtful offense between them, they can climb out of such common problems and even marriage's deepest pit — divorce.

HOW DID I GET DOWN HERE ANYWAY?

I have discovered when a man treats his wife carelessly, she is offended in a way far deeper than he realizes. She begins to close him out and if he continues to hurt her feelings, she will separate herself from him mentally, emotionally, and physically. In other words, she doesn't want any contact in any way with him. Haven't you noticed how your wife clams up after you have insulted her? She not only avoids conversation, but she also avoids being touched. *A wife simply will not respond to her husband* when he continually hurts her feelings without ''clearing the slate.''

Some people justify their reactions by saying, "But he hurt my feelings." There's no such thing as hurt feelings, according to psychologist, Dr. Henry Brandt. He says, let's call hurt feelings what they really are — anger. It may not be right for your wife to react in anger, but that's not the point of this book. Our goal as husbands should be to adjust our behavior so our wives won't have to react in anger.

To understand why your wife naturally "clams up" when you offend her, imagine yourself the proud owner of a new car. When you first drive that classy model into your driveway, every part of you says, "I love it." You love the smell, the feel, the look. Because of your love for the car, you polish it until it sparkles. You devote special time and care to it. When the engine starts knocking, or the oil leaks, the gleaming paint job suffers a few scratches or the windshield wipers quit right in the middle of a rain storm, you become irritated with this "lemon" that you've bought. Soon you can think of seventy-two reasons to get rid of it. As long as it treats you right, you like it. But as soon as it starts to fall apart, you wish you'd never bought it, and soon you don't even want to be near it. You feel ripped off.

The same thing can happen with a job. Did you ever quit because you weren't happy with the boss or working conditions? I remember how much I loved one job until the boss offended me deeply. At that moment, my mind became tangled in a web of reasons to leave. Although I knew what was going on inside me, I couldn't seem to control my emotions. They had changed, and I wasn't as fond of the work as I had been. I eventually didn't want to show up or have anything to do with that job.

We tend to follow a natural pattern when we've been offended. Mentally, we are more alert to the flaws of the offender. Emotionally, we feel estranged. Physically, we feel like avoiding that person.

I have watched my wife go through this process many times. When I played basketball Valentine's evening instead of going home to her romantic candlelight dinner, she was so angry that she didn't want to talk to me. She didn't want to touch me or have me touch her. Have you ever put your arm around your wife after provoking her and felt her tighten up? You may have been tempted to criticize her when that happened, but you need to accept the responsibility for her coldness and say, "I understand how you feel and I don't blame you for not wanting me near you right now." If your wife does not want you to touch her, if she has lost some of that romantic "spark" she once had for you, or if she is plotting ways to get away from you even for short periods of time, *you can be sure you have offended her.*

A wife can be offended anytime or any place. A not so funny thing happened on the way to a party one evening. Norma teasingly said she planned to play a joke on the company president, a joke that would have embarrassed me. I couldn't believe she would consider such a thing and I said, "Norma, you can't do that. I'm not going tonight if you really plan on doing it."

I stopped the car and with harshness and impatience yelled, "I would be too embarrassed to go there." She kidded around with me a little more and admitted she really wasn't serious, but my persistent harshness was too much for her. Because I was so abusive she began to cry. Realizing I had done the wrong thing, I tried to make it right. The more I talked, the worse it grew. At the party, whenever I glanced at her she looked away. She was thinking of all the reasons her husband wasn't such a "good guy" anymore. It took days for me to re-establish harmony.

What does a man have to do to clear up offenses against his wife? How can he maintain harmony with her?

Harmony can be defined as the absence of unsettled offenses between the two of you. When a real harmony and oneness exists between you and your wife, the two of you will want to relax and spend time talking. Your wife will be more agreeable. She will feel emotionally and physically attracted to you. But when you have offended her, mentally, she will probably *resist* you and *argue* with you.

Wives are often accused of being strong-willed and rebellious when, in reality, they're simply responding to their husbands' thoughtless abuses. They are sometimes accused of wrecking marriages because they have lost affectionate or romantic love for their husbands. Of course, husbands seldom realize that their insensitive behavior is what ushered the affection out the door.

Many a man has labeled his wife sexually frigid for not wanting to be touched or have sex. But wives have often told me that when a woman is mistreated, she feels like a prostitute having physical relations with her husband. Sex is more than just physical — it involves every part of us. A woman must first feel valued as a person and be in harmony with her husband before she can give herself freely in sex. Her mind has to believe this man is a worthy "conquerer." Emotionally she has to feel romantic love before *wholeheartedly* entering the sexual union in marriage. Without harmony, the sexual relationship between husband and wife will most certainly deteriorate.

Have you ever known the futility of trying to reach a woman mentally, emotionally, and physically after offending her? The next story illustrates that.

Gary tried to reach out to Laurie, his estranged wife, but she wanted no part of him. He kept saying to her, "I miss you so much. I want to be near you. I love you," but she was *closed* to him emotionally. "Don't you see how you're hurting our daughter?" he said. "Don't you see what kind of reputation we're going to have by being separated?" He tried to appeal to her mentally, but she wouldn't listen. He had already gone too far, so she completely shut him out of her life.

I asked him, "Are you willing to forego touching her for the time being, to forget wondering if she will ever again have emotional feelings for you, to forget trying *to reason* with her mentally? Will you concentrate on clearing up your past offenses?" If Gary would accept my counsel and re-establish a harmony with her, she would mentally open up to him again. Emotionally, she'd start to gain new romantic love for him. Finally, she would desire to be near him again.

"This is the law of life," I advised Gary. "In cases where a woman has fallen in love with another man or has been *severely* mistreated, it may take a little longer to win her back.

A man often becomes disgusted when his wife doesn't sparkle with romance anymore, not knowing he killed that sparkle by his hurtful ways. What steps can a man take to rebuild a harmonious relationship with his wife?

FIVE WAYS TO BUILD A LASTING AND LOVING RELATIONSHIP WITH YOUR WIFE

1. *Endeavor to understand the ways you have offended your wife.* To help you avoid hurting your mate, we have included a list of more than a hundred ways a husband commonly offends his

wife. (This list is included toward the end of the chapter.) In the past, perhaps you haven't realized how your actions were hurting her.

Ken and Sharon's story is a good example of how man's insensitivity damaged a marriage. After eight years of marriage and three children, Sharon's once petite figure was now a little on the chubby side. Since Ken couldn't understand why she had not regained her slender figure after the birth of their third child, he found a number of "creative" ways to point out the extra poundage to Sharon. He tried to make her lose weight by lecturing, demanding, and bribing. He even threatened to cancel their vacation unless she lost weight. But nothing worked. She seemed powerless to comply. Neither she nor Ken realized the physiological reasons women tend to gain weight more easily than men. (Chapter One)

Ken's continually critical, harsh attitude wounded Sharon. As a result, she slowly began to close him out of her life. She resisted when he demanded sex, excusing herself because of headaches or fatigue. She shut him out emotionally because of his occasional jabs, "Do you realize you had two desserts for dinner tonight?" He was unaware that his over-bearing personality continually pressured her, making her more nervous and increasing her desire to eat. (Ken had always assumed people lost their appetites when nervous like he did.) So there was no way he could really understand her. "If you want to lose weight," he said, "you just decide and do it!"

Since Sharon had little or no interest in pleasing Ken, she might have been subconsciously punishing him by staying overweight. Quite by accident, Ken did one thing that finally motivated Sharon to lose weight. He called her long distance while on a business trip and said, "I've been a lousy husband to treat you the way I have. From now on, I'm going to love you — you alone, no matter what."

Sharon responded, "You know, every time you demanded that I lose weight, your attitude was so pitiful that if anything, I wanted to run to the refrigerator and empty it out. I never had any desire to please you. But now that you say I'm free to do whatever I want and I sense you mean it, I actually have a greater desire to lose weight."

Ken became more sensitive and gentle when Sharon explained she really didn't want to be overweight. She felt ugly around her friends and the new fashions only made her look *fatter*. Sharon had said so many times, "If only you would accept me for who I am instead of demanding that I be slender and sexy. . .your rejection is almost more than I can take."

She evidently reacted this way because rejection is one of the deepest pains a human can suffer. It cuts right to the core. When Ken began to recognize the way his criticism had wounded his wife, he was on the right path toward a restored relationship.

2. *Admit your major part in weakening the marriage*. I saved this important point until now because I wanted only those who are very serious about strengthening their marriage relationships to read it. I'm about to describe to you the most bitter medicine I have ever known men to swallow. When I first heard about it from my very dear friend, Ken Nair from California, I resisted it so much because I thought he was crazy. I couldn't believe he was telling me what I'm about to say to you. I squirmed and kicked, fought, and argued for an entire month. In spite of my initial opposition, I ultimately became a "believer" because I have not been able to come up with a single exception to this rule. I have spent long hours laboring to think of an exception. You may think you have the exception, but don't be sure.

I want you to experience whatever emotions would be natural to you as you read the statement in the box below. If you react, I will understand.

> IF A COUPLE HAS BEEN MARRIED FOR MORE THAN FIVE YEARS, THE PERSISTENT DISHARMONY IN THEIR MARRIAGE RELATIONSHIP IS USUALLY ATTRIBUTABLE TO THE HUSBAND'S LACK OF GENUINE LOVE.

I am not suggesting that the husband is solely responsible for all disharmony in marriage. Some day-to-day conflicts may be the result of his wife's physical exhaustion, health problems, over-extended schedules, etc. On any given day, she may respond negatively to her husband due to a headache, a disturbing phone call from her father, or a hormonal change. Certainly, the husband is not to blame for these occasional problems. However, I have found that after five years of marriage, a husband can eliminate prolonged disharmony in his marriage by knowing his wife's needs and meeting them on a consistent basis.

This is very hard to believe, isn't it? But I still can't believe it could be as hard for you to accept as it was for me. It took me months to even imagine that it was true.

During a lecture one man reacted to this concept violently, saying, "When a woman gets out of line, I think you ought to knock her up against the wall."

"Throw him out!" a woman in the meeting shouted.

His reaction took me by surprise at first, but I later discovered he and his wife were in one of those "marriage pits." Since he was trying to convince his wife that all the problems in their marriage were *her* fault, accepting my statement would have destroyed his line of reasoning.

I know of at least three types of men who resist swallowing this concept:

1.   A man whose wife has left him. He would have to admit the failure of the marriage was his fault. That admission is almost too much to ask of him.
2.   A man with relatives or close friends whose wives have divorced them. "It couldn't have been my brother's fault. You never met his terrible wife." Don't forget though, most of what you know about that "terrible wife" you learned from your brother.
3.   A man having an affair. It is just too hard for him to blame himself for a frigid or nagging wife. He feels she was enough to drive him into another woman's arms.

I tried in vain to find an excuse to get out of this *principle* with the phrase, "What would happen *if.* . ?" Don't follow my example. If you base your objection to this principle on hearsay or hypothetical situations, *your* objection is unfounded. Before you excuse any husband, you have to hear both sides of the story firsthand, and the story can't be fiction.

No matter what lurks in our past years of marriage, we need to start applying the principles that can build our present relationships. I believe that as husbands we ought to start anew today.

IT SOUNDS ONE-SIDED, DOESN'T IT?

I knew by Norma's facial expression that I had offended her one morning. I immediately said, "I understand what I just said was too harsh, and I shouldn't have said it. I would like to ask you to forgive me."

"Okay, I'll forgive you," she said.

I thought to myself, "You know this whole thing is one-sided here. It seems like all the pressure is on me to act right. What about her?"

So I said, "Hey, how come I'm always the one that has to ask forgiveness when I do something wrong? Why don't you ask me to forgive you anymore? This is one-sided, isn't it?"

Then she looked at me and said, "I'd be happy to admit where I was wrong and seek your forgiveness *if* I have offended you."

"Well that's just too much! What an arrogant statement. What a terribly selfish thing to say," I said. "There are lots of things you have done to offend me. I can't remember the last time you admitted you were wrong and sought my forgiveness."

"Well, what are some of my offenses?" she asked.

"Give me a minute and I'll think of a lot of them," I said.

"Well, what are they?" she asked again.

"Just a minute and I'll think of some," I said stalling for time.

I thought and thought, but I couldn't come up with even one. I told myself, "This can't be true." But I couldn't think of a thing she had done to offend me where she needed to seek forgiveness.

Finally I said, "But I can think of some things I'd like to see you change about yourself."

"Well, what are they?"

"Even though we've been married five years, I'm going to come up with the first exception to this thing of it being all my fault." (I was pleased with myself.) "There are some times when you don't respect me and you don't honor me as a special person in your life. Sometimes your words are cutting and disrespectful. . .*now how is that my responsibility?*"

We sat down at the kitchen table and started going through each item. It took only ten minutes for us to figure out that every time she had been disrespectful to me I had either rolled out of bed grouchy or been critical of her most of the day. I hadn't earned her respect. It was amazing. All three things I had felt she should change were a direct result of my failure to love her in a genuine way.

Now I have to admit the whole episode left a bad taste in my mouth. Even today, when I'm tired or a little down, I think to myself, "This is crazy. I shouldn't even tell people this because it'll make wives run all over their husbands." But just the opposite is true. When a man treats his wife with gentleness, if he is loving and understanding, and if he does most of the things we describe in this book, she will respond to him on every level. She'll desire intimate conversation with him, she'll feel emotional love for him, and she'll respond to him sexually. The only exception, as I mentioned before, occurs when a wife is romantically involved with another man.

I know how *hard* it is to admit we are wrong. One night Norma and I were lying in bed when I said something obnoxious to her. She closed me out, and though I wanted to restore our relationship, I was too proud to say anything. The words stuck in my throat. I wanted to say, "Norma, I was wrong about what I just said." I tried, but it just wouldn't come. So I decided to go to sleep, thinking in the morning it would be easier to admit my mistake. Throughout the night, I woke up and felt more and more eager to admit my wrong and worse about what I had done. By morning, I could admit my mistake and our relationship was restored. But do you realize what I did to her all night long? I let her suffer with the feelings of a broken relationship.

3. *Express sorrow to your wife whenever you offend her.* My wife has told me time and time again how much she appreciates seeing my genuine sorrow when I have hurt her. "How do you put up with me? How do you live with me? You deserve the medal of honor for staying with me. You deserve the purple heart. You are an amazing woman to live with such an insensitive man." Sincere

words like those express my repentant spirit and soothe our relationship.

I asked a wife, "After your husband has verbally abused you, would you appreciate it if he admitted he was wrong and expressed sorrow that you were hurting? What would you do if he said, 'How do you put up with such a crumb like me, as insensitive as I am?' "

"I'd call the cops," she said.

I repeated her answer in amazement, "You'd call the cops?"

"Yes, because I'd know that there was an imposter in the house," she replied.

I have had wives say to me, "My husband will never admit when he's wrong. He's too proud." Yet I meet husbands everywhere who are willing to admit their offenses if their wives are patient enough to help them understand *how* they have offended them.

4. *Seek her forgiveness for your offensive behavior.* A woman needs a man who *understands* the *depth* of her grief after his hurtful behavior. Wives have said to me, "If only my husband knew how much I feel those words that he says so glibly and harshly. If only he knew how long they stay with me." Harsh words can stay with a woman for years. If a man knew the depth of her feelings, he would try to avoid them at all cost.

A woman loves to hear her man say, "Will you forgive me?" And when she verbalizes, "Yes, you're forgiven," she is freer to restore her side of the relationship. However, if her husband simply says, "Oh honey, I'm sorry," it's not always enough. He might be able to get away with it if he says it in a tender and gentle way. But a woman really needs to hear, "Will you forgive me?" That proves her husband values her half of the relationship. A flippant "I'm sorry" may mean "I'm sorry I got caught" or "I'm sorry I have to put up with your insensitivity." It usually doesn't restore the relationship to oneness and harmony.

5. *Let her see your consistent and sincere efforts to correct offensive actions or words.* A woman isn't impressed with a man who seeks forgiveness or admits he is wrong and then continues

to hurt her year after year in the same areas. Words are nice, but they are not enough.

Attitudes, not words or actions, often harm a woman the most. When she *sees* her husband's attitudes changing, she is more willing to open herself to him and accept him into an intimate relationship. Otherwise, she'll keep him closed off for fear of being offended again.

CAN A WEAKENED MARRIAGE RELATIONSHIP REALLY BE TRACED TO THE HUSBAND'S LACK OF GENUINE LOVE?

I want to emphasize the fact that only after *five* years of marriage is a husband responsible for the prolonged disharmony in his marriage. When you marry a woman, you inherit the way she was treated by her father, her mother, her brothers and sisters, and even her playmates. She is the sum total of her environment, her associations, and the difficulties she faced as a single girl.

The main problem that we men have to overcome is our *lack* of knowledge and skills to *restore* our wives to a level on which we can enjoy a growing, loving, and intimate relationship with them.

You may be thinking thoughts similar to those Mike had when he challenged me on this whole concept. I am regularly challenged, and I challenge it myself from time to time.

"Now wait a minute," Mike said. "That can't be true."

I assured him, "I know, it's hard to believe."

"Well, take my wife, Carol, for example," he said. "She has divorced me, but you can't tell me that the problems we had in our relationship can all be traced to my failure to love her. I just can't buy that."

To prove my point, I said, "Give me an example — something you didn't like about her — and we'll see if we can check this thing out."

"Take this one example," he said, confident that he could disprove this concept. "On our wedding night we had sexual relations. She was turned off by the whole experience and from that day on, for over twenty years, she never really enjoyed our sex life. She never initiated it. She didn't even want to be involved. It was always at my initiative.

"I felt she was more of an object that wasn't really involved in this relationship. How would I be the cause of that? On our wedding night, she changed on me!"

Mike had dated Carol for three years. I asked him how he treated her during those years.

"Well, okay," he said.

"Mike, I happen to know that it wasn't okay. You and I both know that you had a reputation of being mean and extremely insensitive to her. Do you remember some of the things you did?"

When he admitted that he did remember, I said, "You really hurt her feelings. All those days that you dated her, did you ever clear up your offenses with her?"

"No, I didn't. I didn't know how to do it. I didn't know what to do," he said.

"Why did she marry you, to get away from her family?"

"Right."

"The first night she realized that sex wasn't that great, and do you know why?" I asked. "Because you two weren't in harmony. Besides this fact, did you prepare her for sex?" I explained that many women tell me they need as much as three days preparation for sex, romantically and emotionally, before they can respond to their husbands.

"Did you ever clear your conscience with her? Did you ever clear those past offenses when you were married?" I asked him.

"No, I never did." Mike had never admitted he was wrong.

"Did you criticize your wife a lot?" I asked. Mike's head sank lower and lower. He even admitted he once told her all their problems were her fault. After a few nminutes, tears appeared in his eyes because he realized how insensitive, cruel and harsh he had been for all those years.

The upcoming chart on pages (29 - 31) will provide some additional illustrations to help you discover how you might have contributed to a weaker marriage relationship. (This chart was taken from Ken Nair, a marriage and family lecturer/counselor). If you need help you have an expert in your home — your wife. You may be amazed at how well she remembers your unloving words and actions. However, many wives say they are fearful of their husbands, afraid to be honest for fear they'll be *rejected* or *criticized* for being illogical, too sensitive or unforgiving.

IF YOU REACT TO THIS IDEA, YOU'RE NOT ALONE. MANY WIVES AND SINGLE WOMEN JOIN YOU

I explained this concept to an older woman whose husband had left her after many years of marriage for a younger woman. She resisted the idea that I could trace their broken relationship to her husband's failure.

"Oh, this is ridiculous. Everyone knows it's a fifty-fifty deal. I'm just as much responsible as he was," she argued.

"Well, I'm looking for my first exception. I would certainly appreciate it if you would explain to me where you were wrong in the relationship," I told her.

An hour later, she realized that if her husband had treated her differently, she would have responded much differently during those years. We traced everything he had accused her of to his failure to love her.

Some men (including me) have said this material is dangerous because it will make women irresponsible. They panic because they are afraid their wives will accuse them of things they *really are guilty* of in a marriage relationship. I can understand the panic. In general, the concept provokes us to rage because it reveals our irresponsibility as husbands and we just can't take it, especially at first. Believe me, I know and understand the fight that might be going on inside you at this moment.

Some single women also react negatively to this concept at first. For example, I overheard two of my women editors discussing the concepts in the book; one was single and the other married.

"I just can't believe that some of the ideas in that book are good," said Debi, a twenty-five-year-old single woman. "I don't believe part of it, like women are more emotional."

"Just wait until you're married," Judy told her. "In a year and a half of marriage, my husband and I have run into many of the problems discussed in the book."

"Some of the generalizations bother me, though," Debi continued. "I don't feel that women in general are more sensitive and men more logical. I don't think you're more sensitive, because I've seen you at work. I know you."

"But it's different in a marriage," Judy said. "Just the other day when my husband was reading a chapter I had edited, he said, 'Hey, I think you're letting your thoughts creep into this book!' because the example was almost an identical account of a discussion we had recently."

Later Debi told me of an experience with her boyfriend that made her more aware of the differences between men and women. She was extremely tired one day and frustrated because several aspects of her job irritated her. Instead of comforting her with understanding and a gentle embrace, her boyfriend lectured her on how she should have taken better care of herself.

If this section of the book doesn't do any more than stimulate you to try and find an exception to the rule, it will be worthwhile. If five years from now, we discover hundreds of exceptions, the experience will not do much damage because you and I as husbands need to become more responsible, loving partners no matter what our wives do. That is the basis for genuine love — *doing what is right no matter what the other person does or says.*

The motivation in genuine love is to build a relationship primarily for the other person's sake and when we do that, *we* gain because *we* have a better relationship to enjoy.

Listed below are the one-hundred *plus* ways a husband can offend his wife. When a husband recognizes that he has offended her in any one of these ways, he needs to clear it up to restore the relationship. Why not ask your wife to check the ones that are true of you?

1. Ignoring her.
2. Not valuing her opinions.
3. Showing more attention to other people than to her.
4. Not listening to her or understanding what she feels is important.
5. Closing her out by not talking or listening to her (the silent treatment).
6. Being easily distracted when she's trying to talk.
7. Not scheduling special time to be with her.
8. Not being open to talk about things that you do not understand.
9. Not being open to talk about things that she does not understand.

10. Not giving her a chance to voice her opinion on decisions that affect the whole family.
11. Disciplining her by being angry or silent.
12. Making jokes about areas of her life.
13. Making sarcastic statements about her.
14. Insulting her in front of others.
15. Coming back with quick retorts.
16. Giving harsh admonitions.
17. Using careless words before you think through how they will affect her.
18. Nagging her in harshness.
19. Rebuking her before giving her a chance to explain a situation.
20. Raising your voice at her.
21. Critical comments with no logical basis.
22. Swearing or using foul language in her presence.
23. Correcting her in public.
24. Being tactless when pointing out her weaknesses or blind spots.
25. Reminding her angrily that you warned her not to do something.
26. Having disgusted or judgmental attitudes.
27. Pressuring her when she is already feeling low or offended.
28. Lecturing her when she needs to be comforted, encouraged or treated gently.
29. Breaking promises without any explanation or without being asked to be released from the promise.
30. Telling her how wonderful other women are and comparing her to other women.
31. Holding resentment about something she did and tried to make right.
32. Being disrespectful to her family and relatives.
33. Coercing her into an argument.
34. Correcting or punishing her in anger for something for which she's not guilty.
35. Not praising her for something she did well, even if she did it for you.

36. Treating her like a little child.
37. Being rude to her or to other people in public, like waitresses and clerks.
38. Being unaware of her needs.
39. Being ungrateful.
40. Not trusting her.
41. Not approving of what she does or how she does it.
42. Not being interested in her own personal growth.
43. Being inconsistent or having double standards. (Doing things you won't allow her to do.)
44. Not giving her advice when she really needs it and asks for it.
45. Not telling her occasionally that you love her.
46. Having prideful and arrogant attitudes in general.
47. Not giving daily encouragement.
48. Failing to include her when you are with other people.
49. Failing to spend quantity or quality time with her when you're at a party.
50. "Talking her down" — continuing to discuss or argue a point just to prove you're right.
51. Ignoring her around the house as if she weren't a member of the family.
52. Not listening to what she believes is important as soon as you come home from work.
53. Ignoring her at social gatherings.
54. Not attending church as a family.
55. Failing to express honestly what you think her innermost feelings are.
56. Showing more excitement for work or other activities than for her.
57. Being impolite at mealtime.
58. Having sloppy manners around the house and in front of others.
59. Not inviting her out, just the two of you, on special romantic dates from time to time.
60. Not helping her with the children just before mealtimes or times of extra stress.
61. Not volunteering to help her after the meal with the dishes

or with cleaning the house.

62. Making her feel stupid when she shares an idea about your work or decisions that need to be made.

63. Making her feel unworthy for desiring certain furniture or insurance or other material needs for herself and the family.

64. Not being consistent with the children; not taking an interest in playing with them and spending quality and quantity time with them.

65. Not showing public affection for her, like holding her hand or putting your arm around her (you seem to be embarrassed to be with her).

66. Not sharing your life with her, like your ideas or your feelings (Ex., What's going on at work).

67. Not being the spiritual leader of the home.

68. Demanding that she submit to you.

69. Demanding that she be involved with you sexually when you are not in harmony.

70. Being unwilling to admit you were wrong.

71. Resisting whenever she shares one of your "blind spots".

72. Being too busy with work and activities.

73. Not showing compassion and understanding for her and the children when in real need.

74. Not planning for the future, making her very insecure.

75. Being stingy with money, making her feel like she's being paid a salary, and not much at that.

76. Wanting to do things that embarrass her sexually.

77. Reading sexual magazines in front of her or the children.

78. Forcing her to make many of the decisions regarding the checkbook and bills.

79. Forcing her to do some of your dirty work with bill collectors and overdue bills.

80. Not letting her lean on you from time to time in gentleness and strength.

81. Not allowing her to fail but always feeling like you have to lecture her.

82. Refusing to let her be a woman.

83. Criticizing her womanly characteristics or sensitivity as being weak.
84. Spending too much money and getting the family too far into financial debt.
85. Not having a sense of humor and not joking about things together.
86. Not telling her how important she is to you.
87. Not sending her special love letters from time to time.
88. Forgetting special dates like anniversaries and birthdays.
89. Not defending her when somebody else is complaining or tearing her down especially if it's one of your relatives or friends).
90. Not putting your arm around her and hugging her when she's in need of comfort.
91. Not bragging to other people about her.
92. Being dishonest.
93. Discouraging her for bettering herself, her education or her health.
94. Continuing distasteful habits like coming home drunk.
95. Not treating her as if "Handle With Care" were stamped on her forehead.
96. Ignoring her relatives and the people who are important to her.
97. Taking her for granted, assuming that "a woman's work is never done" around the house.
98. Not including her in future plans until the last minute.
99. Never doing little unexpected things for her.
100. Not treating her like an intellectual equal.
101. Looking at her as a weaker individual in general.
102. Being preoccupied with your own goals and needs, making her feel like she and the children do not count.
103. Threatening never to let her do something again because she made some mistake in the past.
104. Criticizing her behind her back. (This is really painful for her if she hears about your criticism from someone else.)
105. Blaming her for things in the relationship that are clearly

your failure.

106. Not being aware of her physical limitations, treating her like a man by rough-housing with her or making her carry heavy objects.

107. Losing patience or getting angry with her when she can't keep up with your schedule or physical stamina.

108. Acting like you're a martyr if you go along with her opinions.

109. Sulking when she challenges your comments.

110. Joining too many organizations which exclude her and the children.

111. Failing to repair items around the house.

112. Watching too much TV and therefore neglecting her and the children.

113. Demanding that she sit and listen to your point of view when she should be taking care of the children's needs.

114. Insisting on lecturing her in order to convey what you believe are important points.

115. Humiliating her with words and actions, saying things like "I can't stand living in a pig pen."

116. Not taking the time to prepare her to enjoy sexual intimacy.

117. Spending money extravagantly without helping those less fortunate.

118. Avoiding family activities that the children enjoy.

119. Taking vacations that are primarily for your pleasure, like fishing or hunting, while preventing her from shopping and doing the things that she enjoys doing.

120. Not letting her get away from the children just to be with friends, go shopping for special items, or have a weekend away with her friends.

121. Being unwilling to join her in the things she enjoys like shopping, drinking coffee in a restaurant, etc.

122. Not understanding the boring chores a wife does:
   • picking up clothes and toys all day long
   • wiping runny noses
   • putting on and taking off muddy boots and jackets
   • washing and ironing
   • etc., etc.

ADDITIONAL ILLUSTRATIONS ON HOW A HUSBAND'S LACK OF GENUINE LOVE WEAKENS A MARRIAGE RELATIONSHIP

WIFE

Wife's Offensive Habits		Amplified
NAGGING	*	Repeatedly reminding her husband about things that need attention with illustrations of his past wrongs.
IMPULSIVE SPENDER	*	She spends money as though it were very easily obtained, seems irresponsible with money when it comes into her possession, uses credit card without concern.
PERMISSIVE ABOUT CHILDREN	*	Makes excuses for children's disobedience to husband and keeps secrets from him about their conduct.
DOMINATING	*	Answers all questions, even those directed to her husband. Makes the decisions in the home and assumes responsibility for disciplining the children.
TOO EMOTIONAL	*	Cries often and is very easily hurt, holds onto hurts for a long time, able to recall past offenses in detail.

HUSBAND

Husband's Lack of Gen. Love		Amplified
UNRELIABLE	*	He lets time slip by unnoticed.
INATTENTIVE	*	Preoccupied with personal concerns.

UNTRUST-WORTHY	* Family's reputation has been damaged by his lack of consideration for others.
UNTRUSTING	* He has an attitude of superiority in finances.
CONDEMNING	* Demanding the control of all money. Won't let wife know about financial status.
	* Feels certain that his wife would bankrupt him if she were given the chance.
ANGRY	* In anger, over-reacts to children & others.
DEMANDING	* Doesn't like to be inconvenienced by family
	* Sets standards too difficult for children to meet.
UNCARING	* Doesn't seem to care about family needs.
IRRESPONSIBLE	* Seems to feel as though the only obligation he has to the family is financial.
INSENSITIVE	* Uses hurtful words to others.
UNKIND	* Uses his wife or others as his source of humor.
THOUGHTLESS	* Dismisses other's personal feelings as unrealistic or not valid, if he acknowledges their reactions at all.

HERE ARE A FEW MORE. . .
CAN YOU IDENTIFY WITH ANY OF THESE TYPICAL CONFLICTS IN MARRIAGE?

Things a Husband Dislikes and Critizes in His Wife:

1. Wants to be with her mother more than me
2. Lazy around the house
3. Sexually frigid
4. Sneaky
5. Overly critical of the way I spend money
6. Avoids doing acitivites with me

7. Makes me feel like a nobody
8. Fear of speaking in front of groups
9. Yelling at the kids in the morning
10. Inflexible, always getting offended in her spirit
11. Independent
12. Rebellious (unsubmissive)
13. Disrespectful
14. Snappy, angry
15. Reacts to my friends
16. Naggy
17. Fearful of moving
18. Talks too much on the telephone
19. Too lenient with the children
20. Reacts to my relatives
21. Too strict with the children
22. Unwilling to pray with me

Common Evidence of Husband's Failure to Love His Wife:

1. Overly critical, non-communicative.
2. Critical of how she keeps the house. Too demanding, perfectionist.
3. Offending her, harsh, demanding, offending the children.
4. Critical, judgmental, harsh, unyielding, insensitive to the needs of the children, stubborn, overly argumentative.
5. Irresponsible with the money, extravagant.
6. Critical, not fun-loving, non-communicative, unwilling to shop or drink coffee with her.
7. Harsh, offended her severely.
8. Critical of her grammer or speaking ability.
9. Undisciplined, neglecting the training of children, not helping her get them off to school . . .
10. Rejecting her, criticizing her.
11. Too possessive, critical of her.
12. Severely offending her and not clearing it up.
13. Harshness, avoiding her to be with other people and things.
14. Severely offending her, broken promises.

15. Preferring your friends over her, defending your friends over her.
16. Not assuming your responsibility, inattentive, untrustworthy.
17. Sudden changes in the past, impulsive.
18. Not talking with her enough.
19. Too strict with the children.
20. Preferring your relatives over her.
21. Too lenient with the children.
22. Offending her.

6

What no woman can resist

The crunch of corn chips distracted my attention from the Saturday afternoon football game. I watched in amazement as my wife and three children began to eat their sandwiches and drink their cokes while I sat only a couple of feet away without a bite to eat.

"Why didn't she make me a sandwich?" I asked myself. "I'm the sole bread winner and I'm being ignored as if I didn't exist." I cleared my throat loudly to catch her attention. When that didn't work, I became so irritated that I walked into the kitchen, got the bread out and made my own sandwich. When I sat back down, she didn't say a word nor did I.

I kept wondering, "If women are so sensitive, how come she didn't know I wanted a sandwich? If women are so alert, why didn't she hear me clear my throat or notice that I wasn't speaking to her? Why didn't she notice the expression of irritation on my face?"

I didn't say anything about it at the time. A few days later when we were talking calmly, I said, "I've really been wondering about something and I hesitate asking you this question. I was really intrigued the other day, and I wonder if I could ask you a personal question?" By now I had aroused her curiosity.

"Sure," she said.

"You know last Saturday when I was watching the football game and you made sandwiches for all the kids? Could I ask you why you didn't make one for me?"

"Are you serious?" she asked. She looked at me with such amazement that it really confused me.

"Sure, I'm serious. I would think that since I'm the one who earns all the money for food around here and you were making the meal, that you would have made me something to eat."

"You know, I really can't believe that you would even ask a question like that," she said. By now, I was wondering, "Maybe I shouldn't have asked, maybe I should know the answer." It seemed very obvious to her but it didn't seem obvious to me at all.

"Norma, I really don't see it and I admit I am blind in some areas," I pursued, "and I can see this is one of them. Would you mind telling me?"

"Sometimes women are accused of being stupid, but we aren't," she answered. "We don't just set ourselves up to be criticized." She seemed to think that explained why she hadn't made me a sandwich.

"I can understand that. But what does that have to do with the sandwiches?"

"Do you realize that every time I make you a sandwich, you say something critical about it? 'Norma, you didn't give me enough lettuce. Is this avocado ripe? You put too much mayonnaise on this. Hey, how about some butter? Well it's a little dry.' "

"Maybe you've never even realized it, but you have had a critical statement for every sandwich I ever made. So not long ago, I just decided that it wasn't worth it. I don't enjoy being criticized."

I had egg all over my face because I could recall all the times I criticized her as she handed me sandwiches. I was simply eating the fruit of my ways. I sowed criticism and reaped an empty plate. I am unhappy to say that after that experience I began praising every sandwich she made for me, and now she gladly makes them for me.

Shortly after Marilyn left Bob, I asked her if she could recall things for which Bob praised her. She couldn't remember a single time during their twenty-plus years of marriage. Her children confirmed it. They agreed that their mother had never served a single dinner that their father didn't criticize in at least one way. He had griped when the salt and pepper wasn't on the table, or when she didn't cook the meat just right. She finally reached the point that she didn't even want to be near his critical personality. She left him for another man.

"I'm kind of happy she's leaving me, because she never wants to do anything with me anyway," Bob said. "She's a party-pooper and a loner. She excludes me from her activities. Do you know she never wanted to go on a vacation with me? I've tried and I've tried, but she never wants to. I'm disgusted with her too."

We didn't discuss his marital problems until after he told me about his job change due to friction with his former boss.

"Tell me how he treated you, Bob," I asked.

"He'd come out to the shop where I was the foreman, and he'd look for one little thing to yell at me about in front of all my men. That really hurt me deeply. Then he would go back to his office and I'd continue working my fingers to the bone. He'd never notice how hard I worked or even say anything positive about it. I couldn't take it anymore so I asked for a transfer."

I asked Bob, "Would you take a vacation with your boss?"

"Are you kidding? That would be the worst thing in the world," he answered.

"How about doing other activities with him?" When he said no, I pointed out how he was just like his boss. His face dropped and tears came to his eyes.

"You're right. No wonder Marilyn never wanted to go anywhere with me. I never think about things she does to please me and I'm always criticizing her in front of the children and our friends."

It was too late. She was already in love with another man. Though he changed drastically and is now much more sensitive to women, his wife divorced him and remarried.

Women need praise. We should be able to understand their need because we, too, want to know that we are of value to other people. One of the ways we know we're needed is when others express appreciation for *who we are* and *what we do*.

Years ago I can vividly remember my boss saying, "If only I had ten men like you, we could change the world." After that, I was so motivated I couldn't do enough for him.

Teachers know how praise motivates children. One teacher said she praised each student in her third grade class every day, without exception. Her students were the most motivated, encouraged, and enthusiastic in the school. When my high school geometry teacher praised me regularly, my "D" average climbed to an "A" in six weeks.

Knowing how significant praise can be, why do we as husbands fail to express it to our wives? Several reasons. The most common is preoccupation with our own needs, vocation, activities. We lose sight of the positive and helpful qualities in our wives when we are preoccupied. Even worse, we fail to acknowledge our wives' helpful traits when we do notice them.

When a husband forgets his wife's need for praise, the marriage is on the way to a breakdown. He just can't get by, ignoring his wife's limitless capacity for praise. And if he fills it with the bitter instead of the sweet, his marriage will become less fulfilling every day. Criticism is devastating to women, especially when voiced in anger or harshness. When a husband rails against his wife for her unique feminine qualities, he conveys a lack of approval for her as a person. It automatically weakens their relationship and can lead to separation.

Charlie Jones, in the book *Life is Tremendous*, says we really can't enjoy life until we learn how to see and say something positive about everything. Though none of us *will ever be completely* positive about life, he says, we can be *in the process* of learning, growing and developing.

If you develop a positive attitude, not only will others want to be around you more often, but your wife will also benefit tremendously. She will have a greater sense of worth and value, knowing you have provided the encouragement only a husband can give.

I believe you would greatly encourage your wife and deepen your marriage relationship by following these simple suggested steps in learning how to praise her.

1. PLAN TO PRAISE HER ONCE A DAY

First, promise yourself to tell her daily what you appreciate about her. Promise yourself — not her — because she might develop expectations and be hurt if you forget. Begin by learning to verbalize your thoughts of appreciation.

Here are some typical statements wives have told me they enjoy hearing:

1. What a meal! The way you topped that casserole with sour cream and cheese. . .M-m-m-m. . .that was delicious."
2. (This next one is great with an early morning kiss.) "Honey, I sure love you. You're special to me."
3. While in the company of friends, say, "This is *my* wife. She's all mine."
4. Put little notes on the refrigerator like, "I loved the way you looked last night."
5. "You're such a dedicated wife to make my lunch every day."
6. "Our kids are really blessed to have a mother like you. You take such good care of them."
7. "I don't know if I prefer the dress or what's in it better."
8. "Do I like your hairstyle? I'd like any hairstyle you have just because it's on you."
9. "I'd love to take you out tonight just to show you off."
10. "Honey, you've worked so hard. Why don't you sit down and rest for awhile before dinner? I can wait."
11. "Tonight, let me finish dinner and feed the kids. You take a bubble bath to relax and I'll get the kids started on their homework."

Margaret Hardisty, in her book *Forever My Love*, emphasized that women tend to approach life on an emotional plane while men approach it on a more logical, sometimes coldly objective one. Therefore, in order to praise your wife, it's more important to use words and actions that communicate praise *from her point of view*. Anything that is romantic or deals with building deeper relationships usually pleases wives.

2. BE CREATIVE WHEN YOU PRAISE

One husband lost his wife and won her back partly through creative praise. He bought 365 pieces of wrapped candy, wrote a special message on every wrapper, and then sealed them again.

She opened one piece every day and read what he appreciated about her for a full year.

A woman loves to find hidden notes, in her jewelry box, the silver drawer, the medicine cabinet. . .Search for ways to praise your wife. The possibilities are endless.

What kind of praise would you like to hear from your boss? Try a little of it on your wife. You may say, "Well, I don't need too much praise. I'm secure in my job and I really don't need it." Then interview some of those who work with you to see how they would appreciate being praised. Some of their ideas might work with your wife. Also, interview your wife and ask her what kind of praise she likes to hear.

DON'T DRAW ATTENTION TO HER UNATTRACTIVE FEATURES

Wrinkles, gray hair, and excess weight are definitely not on the list of possible conversation starters. Even your casual comments about them can make your wife insecure — she may fear being traded in on a "newer model". She knows divorce is just too easy and common nowdays.

One husband wrote his wife a cute poem about how much he loved her little wrinkles and that he loved carressing her "cellulose cells." His card, though softened with flowers, made her cry for hours. Men, we have to praise our wives without drawing attention to their unattractive features.

That doesn't mean insincere flattery. Have you ever been to a party where someone compliments you and you know inside they didn't mean what they said? Sometimes a husband will casually remark, "Oh yeah, I really like that dress." But his wife can generally detect his insincerity. Even if you don't like her dress, you can say something sincere like, "Honey, the dress isn't half as good looking as you are."

Did you know you can even find something to praise in your wife's faults? The chart on the next page can get you started on finding the positive aspects in the things you consider her "flaws."

HOW TO PRAISE YOUR WIFE FOR HER "FAULTS"

Wife's fault	How her faults are expressed in positive ways
1. Nosy	She may be very *alert* or sociable.
2. Touchy	She may be very *sensitive*. This trait is helpful in raising the children and in helping a husband understand how he offends the children.
3. Manipulating	She may be a very *resourceful* person with many ideas and creative ways to manage the home.
4. Stingy	She may be very *thrifty* in spending money for food and clothing.
5. Talkative	She may be very *expressive* and dramatic.
6. Flighty	She may be an *enthusiastic* person with *cheerful* vitality.
7. Too serious	She may be a very *sincere* and *earnest* person with strong convictions.
8. Too bold	She may be a woman with *strong convictions, uncompromising* with her own standards. (Things are right or wrong to her.)
9. Rigid	She may be a *well-disciplined* person with strong convictions.
10. Overbearing	She may be a very *confident* person — sure of herself.
11. A dreamer	She may be very *creative* and imaginative.
12. Too fussy	She may be very *organized* and efficient.

Specific praise is far better than *general* praise. For example, "That was a great dinner" doesn't do near as much for her as, "The asparagus with the nutmeg sauce was fantastic. I've never eaten anywhere that asparagus tasted so good. I don't know how you can take plain ordinary vegetables and turn them into such mouthwatering delights."

"You're a great Mom", won't send her into orbit, but this might, "I'm really grateful that I married a woman who is so sensitive that she knows just the perfect way of making our kids feel important. They're sure lucky to have such a sensitive mother."

There is no right or wrong time to praise your wife. She'll love it when you're alone, and at other times when you're with your children and friends. Make sure you don't limit your praise to public or private times. If you only praise her in public, she might suspect you're showing off for your friends. If you only praise her in private, she may feel you're embarrassed about it.

Whenever you praise her, it's important that your full attention be on her. If she senses that your mind or feelings are elsewhere, your praise will be less meaningful to her.

As you learn how to praise your wife genuinely and consistently, you'll begin to see a new sparkle in her eyes and new life in your relationship.

TWO WAYS TO TALK ABOUT PRAISE WITH YOUR WIFE

1. *Learn to "prime the pump."*

Husband	What kind of praise do you really enjoy receiving from people?
Wife	Oh, I don't know, just as long as it's sincere I'll like it.
Husband	Do you feel I praise you enough?
Wife	I think so.
Husband	(priming the pump) How about last week's meals? Would you appreciate it if I let you know more often how much I enjoy your cooking?
Wife	Oh, yes, I remember I went to a lot of extra effort on two meals last week and you didn't even mention it. . .

(Now you've got the water flowing). If you can take it, let her go. Show your *concern* and *understanding* by saying things like, "That must really hurt you. You deserve a medal for putting up with me." Comfort her and let her get rid of some of those pent up feelings; Otherwise, she may explode later in life at forty or fifty menopause.

2. *Look for the hidden meaning behind her words.*

Husband	Dear, remember last week when I thanked you for the meal? Did I overdo it in front of Steve and Mary?
Wife	Don't worry about it, it was okay.
Husband	Even when I said, "I'm glad we had company over, she's never cooked better."
Wife	Oh yeah, I did feel bad. You made it sound like I don't cook good meals for you unless we have company.
Husband	I thought you might have felt bad. Let's see, what would have been a better way to say it?"

I believe a husband needs to help his wife be as honest and straightforward as possible so he can know where the relationship is strained. So many times I asked Norma during our early married years not to "beat around the bush or play games with me." I needed the real facts in order to adjust my behavior and learn how to be a better husband. I hope you encourage your wife to be as straightforward as possible to build a deeper, more fulfilling relationship.

7

What women admire most about men

"I'm quitting on Monday," Jim yelled as he blasted through the front door. Elaine greeted him quietly and listened to the account of her husband's job flare-up. "My boss finally did it. I'm not working for him anymore," he said. Giving him time and her full attention, she let him vent his frustration. Then when he had poured it all out, she began to help him rethink the situation. She reminded him that he could never replace the ideal working conditions or the six-figure income. Soon Jim had changed his mind. He has told me since then it was the best decision he ever made. Today he enjoys his job better than ever.

When Jim *honored* Elaine's advice, he not only made a wise vocational decision but also a wise marital decision. Her respect and admiration for him greatly increased in response to his openness. As you learn to receive correction openly from your wife, she, too, will feel an increased admiration and respect for you.

The proverb that honor always follows humility is still true today. Humility is an inner attitude which is evidenced by an openness to the ideas and suggestions of others. It is the recognition that we are not all-knowing, that we can make mistakes. Humility encourages us to look forward to each passing year in order to gain more knowledge and understanding.

The inability to accept advice from others can destroy a

relationship. Read how Larry had to learn the hard way to take his wife's correction seriously.

Lynn had tried for ten years to explain to Larry how badly he made her feel, but Larry simply couldn't understand. His first problem was preferring his relatives over his wife. Whenever he and Lynn were around his family, he expected her to change her schedule to fit in with his family's. It didn't matter what she had planned. If his family wanted to go to the circus, she had to go too. To make matters worse, Larry always took their side over hers and defended them during arguments.

Larry's other fault was his habit of making more commitments than he was able to fulfill. A promise here and a promise there, he was often guilty of forgetting his commitments. He didn't mean any harm. In fact, his intentions were quite good. He wanted so much to make people happy that he couldn't say no when asked to do something. He would promise to do things without realizing there weren't thirty hours in a day.

Year after year, Lynn tried to think of creative ways to point out these two problems to Larry, but nothing seemed to get through to him. Finally during one particularly straining visit to their hometown, Lynn broke down and cried. She openly expressed dislike for his relatives, bringing on Larry's lectures and retaliation. Neither of them could handle the emotional scene, so Larry drove the car to a parking lot. He sat there for nearly an hour, trying to understand the problem, but he simply couldn't. (While we husbands sit puzzled about the cause of the problem, our wives often assume we deliberately offended them.) Larry and Lynn tried to discuss their problem once again as they began the long drive home. Lynn finally hit just the right combination of words that made sense to Larry.

"Oh, so that's why you don't like my relatives," he said. "Now I see why you don't want to move back to our hometown, because when we're with our relatives, I always choose their feelings over yours. You feel second-rate to them. That makes sense now." Lynn was thrilled. One problem down, one to go.

But he remained just as blind to the second problem as he had been to the first. Though Lynn tried to tell him, he finally had to learn it from his friends through a very painful experience. Six of his buddies called a special meeting to tell him about his problem with over-commitment. They had all suffered from his neglect. Graphically, yet lovingly they explained to Larry that his inability to say no was causing them to be resentful toward him. Larry was straining his friendship with each of them. He was so embarrassed and humiliated by this two-hour meeting that his first thought was, "Why didn't I listen to Lynn?"

His wife was relieved to see that he finally understood his second major problem. Her respect for him automatically increased because of his willingness to improve once he finally comprehended his faults. He became eager to expend the effort and study necessary to learn how to love Lynn properly.

Let's set some goals: that we as husbands will be willing to learn the lessons in each chapter, however painful or difficult, and with our new knowledge commit ourselves to building a better marriage. A better marriage doesn't just happen. It takes serious effort channeled in the right direction. The basic principles presented in each chapter, taken one at a time, will correct or prevent the most serious pitfalls we face in marriage.

Some of us entered marriage with an extremely limited knowledge of how to develop a fulfilling relationship with our wives and children. It's not hopeless. With a great deal of teaching and patience on their part, *we can learn*. A man needs to take an honest inventory to assess where he is in his marriage and be able to admit that he might have a long way to go. Your wife and children can certainly help with that inventory.

HOW WOULD YOU DESCRIBE THE IDEAL WIFE?

Can you imagine the ecstatic feeling you would have if your wife volunteered the question, "How can I become a better wife?" The honor you would feel would be overwhelming. Of course, it would be absurd to expect this kind of question to come up between most husbands and wives. But just close your eyes for a moment, lean back in your chair, and visualize your wife asking you such a question. It would be great, wouldn't it? If you want your wife to do this for you, first set the example and work on becoming a better husband. Ask her how you can improve as a husband, a father, and a person. You'll give her new hope for gaining the type of marriage she's always wanted. If she sees that you are sincere, ultimately she'll become far more responsive to your needs and desires.

Do you want to be the type of husband wives and families complain about the most? All you need is an arrogant, all-knowing attitude and an unwillingness to admit when you're wrong. Three tiny words produced such disgust in one wife that she said, "I get sick inside and ask myself, 'Why did I ever marry this man? What a tremendous mess I have gotten myself into.' " What are those three tiny words? "*I'll never change. . .*"

"*I'll never change*," her husband repeated, "so don't try to change me and don't tell me where I need to change. If you think changing is so important then why don't *you* change and just leave me alone. The biggest change our marriage needs is for you to keep your mouth shut!"

Wives tell me they admire and honor a husband who admits when he is wrong, especially when he openly seeks his wife's advice on how to improve. I believe a man needs to *motivate himself* to become more interested in his wife's ideas on how he can improve.

1. WHAT SHE'S REALLY SAYING

First, look for the meaning behind your wife's statements. It is easier to avoid reacting solely to her words if you actively search for the meaning behind them. Have you ever said to your wife, "You're wrong. I don't *always* do that. Don't you think you're exaggerating?" She probably didn't mean "*always*", as in, every single time. That's just her way to emphasize a point. The *wise* husband looks beyond that offensive word and says, "Tell me how you're feeling right now. Tell me some of the thoughts behind what you just said. Tell me why you feel you need to use the word 'always' ". Reassure her that she does not have to explain in detail right away. Ask if she'd like to think about it for a day or two. A genuine learner does not put demands on others, forcing them to comply with his impatient desires immediately. He gives others time to feel, think, and change.

Many a husband has refused to listen to his wife's correction because of logical hang-ups over her choice of words. Words have no meaning apart from the interpretation we each place upon them. It is our responsibility in communicating with our wives to understand their *true* intentions.

A husband's tone of voice and facial expressions will reveal whether he has a sincere motivation to learn. His wife will not be as honest if she perceives her husband is not really serious about learning and changing.

Chapter Ten delves more into deep communication, so I will conclude with this summary: Avoid reacting to the words your wife uses and look for the meaning or intention behind them.

2. LET HER WORDS SINK IN

Let your wife's advice sink in like a good spring rain. Hold off on responding until you have deeply received what she had said. Norma told me for years that I frowned when I said certain things to our children. She told me they felt I was angry with them, that I was rejecting them. My furrowed brow frightened them, she said. "I'm not frowning and I'm not angry," I told her. But after I *took the time* to look in the mirror, I said, "I need to work on that. I appreciate your sharing that with me."

3. HOLD YOURSELF ACCOUNTABLE FOR FAILURE

I used to flick the children with my finger on their foreheads or arms when they misbehaved. If one of them was chewing food with his mouth open, I would reach across the table and flick him on the head and say, "Cut that out." Norma has made me aware of how this belittles and wounds our children. What a degrading thing to be flicked on the head by your father! Besides, it must hurt. It even hurts *my* finger.

I know deep inside that flicking them is not right. Sometimes, right when I do it, Norma will ask, "Kari, how does that make you feel?" Kari replies, "It always makes me feel bad when Dad does it." I finally came up with a way to break myself of this habit. I said to each of the children, "If I flick you on the head in anger or irritation, then I will pay you a dollar for each time I do it." I thought this might work well because I don't like to give money away. Believe me, my kids are alert enough *not* to let one slip by. It's been a long time since I've flicked one of them.

Great memories come from experiences such as this. On one occasion my son Greg came into the house eating a delicious looking chocolate candy bar he had just bought. I asked him for a bite. *It was good.* Then Kari and Michael came in and wanted a bite too. Greg soon wished he hadn't unwrapped his candy in front of us. Little Michael didn't think Greg was too generous with the portions he doled out, so he decided to buy his own. He asked Greg where he bought it and how much it cost, and then with a longing look in his eyes he said, "Dad, would you please flick me? I need a dollar."

4. SEEK HER FORGIVENESS

As I said before, a woman won't set herself up to be hurt. If you have offended her in the past, she won't be eager to share advice or correction in the present. Seek her forgiveness to reestablish the spirit of communication. Her admiration and respect for you will be straightened and maintained by your willingness to admit your wrongs. Since Chapter Five dealt with forgiveness, review it from time to time when you need more help in this area.

5. RECEIVE HER ADVICE WITH GRATEFULNESS

Oh, the bounty of a grateful man — less nagging, more admiration and gentleness from his wife. When a man shows genuine gratefulness for his wife's correction, she feels a greater freedom to be more gentle the next time she corrects him. No need to nag when you have a grateful listener. A wife also admires her husband more when he is willing to thank her for her advice or correction. The only exception is when a wife has been *deeply* hurt by her husband. She needs his time and patience to respond with admiration and gentleness. Don't fall into the pattern of so many husbands who quit trying when they're so close to success.

Continue to look for the meaning behind what your wife says, let it sink in, and establish consequences for your failure. When you continue to thank her for helping you, you will begin to see the dawning of a stronger relationship.

Though the following illustration is the story of a father and son, it can be applied to a husband and wife. Jim's dad was irresponsible in many ways during his son's formative childhood and teen years. He disciplined Jim by kicking him, ridiculing him, scolding him, and slapping him. As a result, his son withdrew in spirit and, consequently, his mind, and emotions also withdrew. He moved out of the house. When I explained to this father how he had crushed his son in the past, he realized he had not only damaged *their* relationship but possibly his son's future relationships. The father recalled several major incidents where he had severely offended his son.

Because he really wanted to have his son back emotionally, mentally and physically, he made an appointment to see him. It took a lot of nerve, but he admitted to Jim that he was wrong and he was sorry for not being the kind of father he should have been. During his confession, he mentioned all the hurtful incidents he could recall.

His son remembered these specific incidents. "But Dad, that's not all." Then for the next few minutes, he reminded his father of all the other things he had done to hurt him. Jim's father was amazed that his son still remembered it all so vividly. They wiped the slate clean for the first time in years.

When you lose your wife due to offenses, she withdraws mentally, emotionally, and physically. But you can learn to draw her back. Just your willingness to learn will help her respond as she becomes secure in the knowledge that you really want to change.

8

If she's not protected, you get neglected

Dan and Janet had been married more than twenty years when he called me in a panic. "Janet's leaving me for another man," he said. He was crushed and bewildered. "Gary, is there anything you can do to help out?"

Dan's main problem with Janet was easily detectable when we met to talk. Let me explain why I believe he lost her by using his hobby as an illustration. He was an avid, meticulous and knowledgeable gardener. Lush flower gardens defined the borders of his well-kept front and back yards. Pruned trees shaded the delicate greenery from the hot summer sun. Dan knew where to plant each variety of flower so it would obtain the proper sunlight and soil. Since each plant had special needs, Dan had taken the time to research those needs so he would know exactly how much fertilizer and other nutrients they required. The results were magnificent. But while his garden was a glorious blaze of harmony in nature, his marriage was wilting from lack of attention. He entered his work and other activities with the same enthusiasm he applied to gardening, which left little time for Janet.

Dan hadn't the faintest idea what Janet's needs were. He had very little knowledge about how to protect her from the "scorching summer sun and wind." Not only did he fail to protect her, he convinced her through his logical arguments that she should handle household responsibilities that she had said were too much for her. Dan had failed throughout their twenty years together to listen to her many, many pleadings for tender protection.

Janet was not only holding down a full-time job, but she was responsible for keeping the finances, cooking the meals, cleaning the house and training the children. She faced many crises alone while Dan was fishing, hunting or cultivating his posies. He could not recognize Janet's need to have a strong and gentle man to lean on, one who would protect her from some of the "dirty work". She needed to be accepted and loved as a person with her own special physical limitations. When Dan repeatedly failed to be the man she needed, she looked elsewhere.

We mentioned in Chapter One that men and women differ in their capacity for physical labor. When a man doesn't understand his wife's limitations or explains them away as laziness, numerous misunderstandings can result. For example, a woman with several small children can be totally exhausted both physically and mentally by five in the afternoon. If her husband doesn't recognize her limitations, he may resent her avoidance of sexual relations at ten or eleven at night when she is genuinely too tired to think of a romantic experience with him.

Sadly enough, women are often made to feel guilty because of their natural, physical limitations. Many times during the early years of our marriage, I demanded that Norma help me move couches and desks as we rearranged or moved to new homes. Though she tried to explain she was too tired or weak, I expected her to be able to do it simply because I was doing it. She often said during those years, "I don't know why you married me, you should have married a man."

I wanted her to learn to handle physical and mental strain. I was afraid to help her. I feared she would take advantage of me by expecting me to do her work as well as my own. But when I treated her tenderly, I was surprised to find that she didn't, and I haven't met a woman who has when she's treated in a loving and gentle way.

Keith was willing to gamble money to see if his wife would take advantage of him. He took his wife to a shopping center for her birthday. He told her he would like to help her buy some clothes but never mentioned the amount she could spent. It was Mary's night out because Keith didn't especially like to shop. Two hours and ten shops later, as his feet began to ache, Keith wondered whether this birthday outing was a good idea or not. "Mary, how do you like this dress? It would look good on you." "No, I don't like it."

Finally they wandered into a very nice shop where Mary found a combination skirt, jacket, blouse and pantsuit that she liked well enough to buy. Though the money was beginning to add up, Keith said, "Mary, look at this. Here's a dress on sale." (A word of caution at this point. A wife many times may be offended when her husband limits her "buying power" to the sale rack.)

Mary liked the dress and tried it on. Keith said, "Why don't you get it?"

"Keith, I shouldn't be spending any more of our money."

"Oh no, go ahead and get it," Keith replied. "I like it. Hey Mary, what do you think of this dress?"

"This is getting ridiculous," Mary protested. But she tried it on when Keith insisted.

At this point, he was beginning to wonder if she would buy every dress that he told her to buy. "Oh, I like this one, Mary."

"Keith, I cannot buy another dress," she said. "This is getting ridiculous. We can't afford all this."

"Ah, what difference does it make?" he asked. "You're more important than all this and even if I have to work extra, I'm happy to do it." He really put the pressure on her to buy the dress.

She replied, "I'm embarrassed, I can't buy another dress. Please let's pay for these and go get something to eat."

"Come on Mary. Would you buy just one more for me? I just want you to be really satisfied."

"Keith, I can't do it," she said.

"Okay, we'll pay for them. I want you to be happy and satisfied."

Keith didn't admit until sometime later that he just wanted to prove that a woman well-treated will not take advantage. He praised her for her thriftiness and caution, proud of her willingness to work with him for the financial security they both desired. Now he never worries that Mary will overspend because he is secure she will look for the right price and the best buy. Their experience has also convinced him Mary will not take advantage of him in other areas of their life.

If you have been stingy and critical of your wife's use of money or your relationship is not as solid as it should be, I advise you *not* to try such an experiment until you have a more meaningful relationship. But if your marriage is strong, and you and your wife are not trying to solve a major conflict, I would encourage you to try the experiment to prove to yourself that your wife won't take advantage when she's treated tenderly.

THREE WAYS TO PROTECT YOUR WIFE AND HELP HER BECOME MORE FULFILLED

1. *Discover where your wife needs protection.*
First, a husband needs to discover areas in which his wife feels vulnerable. Through informal discussions and observations on your part, you can compile mental lists of the major and minor areas where she is frustrated or fearful. Driving a car is one of my wife's fearful or vulnerable areas. Because she was involved in a serious auto accident which killed some good friends in high school, she is naturally very alert to any possible danger when she is driving or even riding in a car. She is cautious when she sees other cars coming; she warns me and I appreciate that. It would only frustrate her if I did not give her the freedom to be cautious, knowing her past circumstances. Another area in which my wife feels vulnerable is driving long distances alone in the winter because she fears the car will break down. When we lived in Chicago, the car broke down twice and she had to accept help from passing motorists. Both she and the children could conceivably have been hurt or abused. Since I am aware of her fear, I don't expose her to driving long distances alone anymore.

What about her physical limits?
Many times a man doesn't realize he treats his wife too roughly. He is unaware that his wife's physical limitations keep her from enjoying roughness even when being playful. One wife told me her husband enjoyed wrestling but didn't realize how much it had injured her in the past. He never intentionally hurt her, but she would find bruises on her arms or the rest of her body after they

had wrestled on the carpet. He was rough with her in other ways too. One night they were in the grocery store when she lingered a little too long in the book section. He was waiting for her in the parking lot with a sack of dog food and other items. When she caught up with him, he said, "No wonder you didn't hurry out here. You're not the one holding all the groceries."

"Well, all right, I'll help you," she said. He playfully threw the sack of dog food at her, hitting her in the stomach so forcefully that it left her gasping for breath. The ride home was silent. As they pulled up in the driveway he said, "The reason I was quiet wasn't because I was mad at you. I was mad at myself for hurting you again." He wanted to make an effort to change his behavior because he realized she needed to be treated with tenderness.

Some women feel if they were more feminine their husbands wouldn't be so rough with them. A wife may conclude, "I'm just too masculine in my mannerisms, because he's treating me like a man."

What about the financial pressures?
A man also needs to be more sensitive in protecting his wife from unnecessary financial stress. Many wives endure a tremendous amount of pressure because of a husband's irresponsibility with finances. To compensate for overspending, a husband may force his mate to work when she would rather be home with the children. In fact, some husbands demand it, feeling "she should do her part." If a woman is home all day, her husband may expect her to handle bill payments and financial bookkeeping for the family because he wonders what she does all day anyway.

He might think, "I work eight hours every day. The least she can do is pay the bills."

If it were just a matter of bookkeeping, this would not be a problem. But when it comes to facing angry bill collectors, juggling figures in a checkbook that won't balance, mounting pressures resulting from insufficient money, decisions over which bill to pay first, and making phone calls to appease businesses, the burden *can* become physically and emotionally too much for a wife. The problem is magnified if the husband appears to be spending money loosely and enjoying himself.

I made this mistake in the early years of our marriage. Norma worked for the Bank of America in California. I logically concluded that anyone working for a bank would obviously be able to take care of the money at home. Since financial matters were a weak point for me at that time, I asked her if she would take that responsibility, which she graciously did for four or five years. One day, though, she came to me in tears, laid the records, the checkbook and all the bills in my lap, and said that she just couldn't handle it anymore. You see, we had two checkbooks between us and only one checking account. I would write a check, hoping the money was in the bank. It was a tremendous pressure on my wife. Today I am very grateful she handed over that responsibility, because it forced me to take more responsibility for the financial well-being of our family.

What about expecting her to do all the cooking?
So many men treat their wives as objects to be used. They don't verbalize it, but they maintain the inward conviction that women should remain in the kitchen cooking or cleaning while they play golf, hunt, or relax in other ways. Have you ever noticed during family get togethers with friends or relatives that women are usually the ones who are expected to work in the kitchen, while the men just shoot the breeze? Little girls many times are trained to watch for the special needs of a male family member. For instance, a mother will say, "Go ask Daddy if he wants a glass of iced tea." But we very seldom see little boys asked to do the same thing.

Think of your wife's special limitations before expecting her to take on *added* responsibilities. Such forethought will avoid extra strain on your relationship and protect your wife's mental, spiritual, emotional, and physical life.

What about her need for rest?
Why is it that some men feel their wives need less sleep than they do? While the husband sleeps, his wife may rise to prepare breakfast and take care of the children. This is certainly true where babies are involved. During our early years of marriage, when my children would cry during the night, I automatically expected my wife to get up and take care of them. And she did. Never did I feel the same compulsion to get up and take care of

the kids. A husband can really make points with his wife if he is tender and alert to her physical limitations. If you see that she cannot handle the lack of sleep, be the leader in taking whatever steps are needed to insure that she gets the sleep she needs.

What about the pressure of the children?
Often my wife has said how much she appreciates the times I take charge of the kids when I come home from work. I get them out from underfoot so she is able to finish dinner peacefully. She is usually grateful for the time to be alone. She likes for me to take them outside to play, into another room for reading, or just to talk to them about whatever topic they choose. After the meal, the children and I often clean the table and wash the dishes to let Norma have some time off. Instead of resenting her need for my help as I once did, I now look forward to helping her as often as I can.

Thoughtful, creative ideas on your part are worth much more than the time they cost. They strengthen your marriage and lift your wife's spirit. One night Jim thrilled Debbie when he asked her to let him cook dinner, set the table, and feed the children. He told her he had a gift he would give her if she let him do those things, a bottle of bath oil. While she took a leisurely bath, he took care of her household chores. It was only a small gift; it just took a bit of Jim's time. But to Debbie, it meant that he cared enough to give something extra of himself.

What about the added pressure of moving!
A move from one city to another is a major step for a woman. It requires that her husband be extra sensitive to her limitations. Many times a woman's emotional and physical endurance is depleted just from normal day-to-day routines. A move obviously adds additional stress, even when the move is welcomed.

What can cause her the most stress?
We as husbands need to be aware of the amount of stress our wives face daily. To aid your wife with stress, you must first be aware of the situations which cause her the most anxiety. To help you, we have included a list from *Holmes Study* which ranks

items from the greatest amount of stress to the least amount of stress. The higher on the list, the greater the stress. Check to see how much stress you and your wife are facing today:

Death of a spouse
Divorce
Marital separation
Jail term
Death of a close family member
Personal injury or illness
Just married
Fired at work
Marital reconciliation
Retirement
Change in health of a family member
Pregnancy
Sex difficulties
Gaining a family member
Business adjustment
Change in financial status
Death of a close friend
Change to a different line of work
Foreclosure of a mortgage or loan
Change in responsibilities at work
Son or daughter leaving home
Trouble with in-laws
Outstanding personal achievement
Wife starts or stops working
Begin or end school
Change in living conditions
Revision of personal habits
Trouble with boss
Change in work hours or conditions
Change in residence
Change in schools
Change in recreation
Change in church activitiy
Change in social activity
Change in sleeping habits

Change in number of family get-togethers
Change in eating habits
Vacation
Christmas
Minor violations of the law

Purpose to protect your wife in any and all areas where she feels fearful or vulnerable. That's the first way to show her how much you cherish her.

2. *Discover how your wife wants to be fulfilled.*
Another way to encourage your wife is to help her become fulfilled as a woman. You can do this by discovering her personal goals in life and helping her reach them if possible. We all love to know that someone is pulling for us, that others cheer when we reach a goal. It makes a woman feel worthwhile and valuable when her husband takes time to help her achieve a personal goal.

From time to time, my wife and I get together on a date, for breakfast out or just a retreat from home. During that time we list our personal goals. We commit ourselves to help each other fulfill those goals. This book is a goal that my wife and I wanted to reach in the next two years. I am amazed we had an opportunity to do it so soon. Since she was as excited about it as I was, I knew it was okay with her for me to take several weeks away from my family to work on our goal.

I feel so satisfied, knowing my wife is committed enough to sacrifice for my goals, that I get excited when I think of helping her with her goals. Since I know she wants to maintain her physical health as best she can, we decided she should join a health spa. To see that she has the opportunity to exercise regularly, I am happy to babysit sometimes so she can accomplish her personal goal of good physical health.

Sit down with your wife and ask her to name some goals. She might want to finish college, study public speaking, learn to sew or cook. Her goals may change as she discovers the real pressures or motives behind them. Maybe she says she wants to go back to school, when all she really wants is a couple of days a week away from the children. By relieving her of some of the pressure, you may help channel her energies in the right direction, helping her to reach her *real* personal goals. I believe it is our responsibility to discover our wives' goals and to understand how they want to fulfill themselves as women. Then we must let them be who they want to be by respecting their unique ambitions.

3. *Discover what personal problems your wife wants to solve.* My wife would like to share with women how to be fulfilled in the home without outside work. Unfortunately, during our early marriage she became timid when speaking to groups, due to another one of my irresponsibilities. I used to correct her grammer or give suggestions on how to improve her teaching methods. Whenever I heard her share in front of groups, I always called her attention to anything I thought was less than perfect. Little did I know that my wife's nature was so sensitive that she eventually stopped speaking in front of groups because of my criticism. It took five years of my praise and encouragement to overcome the wounds I had thoughtlessly inflicted. She is speaking to groups more and more now but is still quite nervous when I am in the audience.

Has your wife ever told you emphatically in the morning that she is going to lose weight. . .and that very same evening she's eating donuts? The worst action you can take as a husband is to remind her of that early morning commitment. However, you can comfort her by saying nothing at all or by putting your arm around her to say, "I love you for what you are, not for what you decide to do." She probably feels disappointed enough about her lack of will power. Knowing she is loved *as she is* will probably boost her self-confidence and strengthen her will power.

In summary, a woman loves to build a lasting relationship with a man who cares about her enough to let her lean on him when she needs comfort. She needs a man who will understand her fears and limitations as a woman so that he can protect her. She feels important when her husband stands up and defends her in the presence of someone who is criticizing her.

Each wife is unique, and the only way you can pinpoint her needs is to discuss them with her. You may want to question your wife to see if she feels that you are protective or helpful enough in the areas below:

The family finances
Raising of the children
Household needs and responsibilities
The future — insurance, family wills
Her own employment and the people with whom she works
Her friends and relatives

You should also endeavor to discover where she would like to be fulfilled as a woman. Ask her to explain two or three goals she has always wanted to accomplish. Then re-evaluate her goals with her each year.

Arguments. . .there's a better way

A simple agreement can eliminate heated arguments between you and your wife. No, it's not a divorce!

It involves a principle that increases the time you and your mate spend discussing important areas WITHOUT that familiar anger and silence routine and it also builds her self-respect.

When my wife and I stumbled upon this principle during a Fourth of July argument six years ago, both of our fuses were getting short. The fireworks show was dull in comparison. I wanted to vacation in Colorado in July; she wanted to go to Florida in August. Since we didn't agree on separate vacations either, the discussion became hotter and hotter with no end in sight. Sizzling, I compared her attitude to some of the more submissive single girls from the office.

"You don't have a calm attitude. Besides that, you're wrong," I said.

"I have never met this 'calm woman' you talk about," she replied angrily. "If you can show me just one, I might consider following her example."

At this point the brainstorm that has helped us avoid heated discussions for six years came to me. I asked Norma if she would be willing to drop the conversation and try an experiment for just two months. If it worked, we'd use it; if not we'd search for another solution.

"Will you not make decisions in the home that affect me and

the rest of the family without my complete agreement?" I asked her. "And I won't make any decisions affecting you unless I have your full consent.''

I didn't know if the experiment would work, but I did know that I was tired of arguments and futile discussions that led nowhere except to tears and angry silence. Since I worked for an organization that taught family harmony, I was desperate to achieve it in my own home. You've heard of the plumber with leaky pipes haven't you?

Many things had to change if we were going to agree to agree. We had to reason together for longer periods of time. We would also be forced to discover the reasons behind each other's comments. I had to search for the meaning behind Norma's words and understand her frame of reference if I hoped to convince her of my point of view. Several of our first discussions ended with the consensus that since we couldn't agree we would just wait. Amazingly enough, many topics seemed to solve themselves or at least their importance seemed to diminish as the days passed.

In spite of the success of our idea, I violated it after two months. Hearing a growing argument between Kari and Greg at the breakfast table one morning, I rushed in to referee just in time to see Greg shove his full plate across the table, spilling all over Kari. I was about to take Greg upstairs for a little discipline when Norma said she disagreed.

"Well, our experiment doesn't apply in every situation," I said, stopping in my tracks. "I can't relinquish my responsibility as Greg's father just because you don't agree. I'm sorry. I'll have to overrule you this time."

After Greg and I had our "little talk," Norma greeted me coldly in the kitchen.

"Well Norma, I had to do what I thought was right," I explained. "I wish we could agree in every situation, but it's not practical."

She replied, "I don't think you took the time to find out the facts."

"I saw all I needed to know."

But I had to admit that I didn't know what Kari had done to provoke Greg. Norma had told Kari to make sandwiches for

Greg. Kari probably didn't want to do it in the first place, so when Greg didn't want the sandwiches, she tried to force them on him.

"Mom told me to make you sandwiches and you're gonna eat 'em," she said.

"You're not my boss. I don't have to eat them," Greg retorted. And to make his point, he pushed the sandwiches away. But the table was slicker than he anticipated and the sandwiches slid into Kari's lap.

I admitted to Greg that I was wrong and apologized. To keep such mistakes from happening in the future, we now hold "court" in our family. Each person can bring in all the witnesses he wants to support his story and obtain all the legal counsel needed from within the family. After all the facts are presented, the family decides who is guilty.

Whenever Norma and I do not agree on something that affects the family, I have been amazed at the number of times her decision has been right. I'm not sure whether she has a hot line to Heaven or what, but somehow she can sense when something is not right. Committing ourselves to agree has brought more harmony and deeper communication than anything else we practice. It has increased my wife's self-worth and eliminated pressure-packed arguments.

Constant disagreement can only weaken a marriage relationship. The next part of the chapter discusses the specific consequences of not agreeing on decisions that affect the family and ways to apply the "agreement" principle to your family.

WHAT HAPPENS WHEN YOU MAKE ALL THE DECISIONS

When a wife is left out of the decision making process, she feels insecure, especially if the decisions involve financial security or living conditions. Her constant state of insecurity spreads like a disease to produce instability in other areas of the marriage.

Steve and Bonney had been struggling to make just enough money to put food on the table. His small business was requiring eighteen hours a day on his part, and she was putting in at least eight hours a day at the office, even though she was seven months pregnant. Steve flew east to show his business ideas to a multimillionaire. The man was impressed and made Steve a generous offer which he accepted in less than five minutes. It was the only "reasonable" course of action.

He could hardly wait to call Bonney and tell her the great news in "logical" order so she could get as excited as he was. He told her, "First, you won't have to work any more. Second, he's giving me twenty percent of the profits (he says I'll be a millionaire in a year). Third, you won't believe how beautiful it is back here, and he's going to pay all of the moving expenses."

Steve was shocked to hear uncontrollable weeping on the other end of the line. At first he thought she was crying for joy (I know it's hard to believe, but he actually thought that).

As soon as Bonney caught a breath between sobs, she had a chance to ask some questions Steve considered totally ridiculous (in fact, he thought her mind had snapped). She asked questions like, "What about our parents?" and "What about our apartment — I just finished the room for the baby?" With her third question, Steve, in all of his masculine "sensitivity," abruptly terminated the phone call. She had the nerve to ask if he'd forgotten she was seven months pregnant.

After giving her an hour or two to pull herself together, he called her back. She had gained her composure and agreed to move back east. She left her parents, her friends, her doctor and childbirth classes, and the nursery she had spent so much time preparing for her first child.

It took Bonney almost eight months to adjust to a change that Steve had adjusted to in minutes. Steve never made his million. The business failed eight days before their baby was born, and they moved again to another place still 3,000 miles from home. Steve eventually learned his lesson, and today he doesn't make any major change unless Bonney is in total agreement. He tries to give her ample time to adjust to other changes as soon as he can foresee them. However, Steve will never forget the loving sacrifices his wife made so many times. He even realizes that questions like "What about our parents?" or "What about the nursery?" can be more meaningful than money.

Husbands can also make their wives feel stupid, inadequate, or like an unnecessary member of the family when they make most of the decisions alone. So many wives are educated and intelligent, yet their husbands treat them as if they don't know anything at all. When a decision comes up in the husband's area of expertise or financial dealings his wife might as well forget about participating as far as he's concerned.

Jerry had to lose money before he would respect his wife's judgment. He had considered a number of ways to invest some of his earnings, from apartments, to real estate, to the stock market. After talking to developers and reading literature, he decided to buy a lake-front lot in a planned retirement community. He reasoned that if he bought the land during the early development stages, it would be worth quite a bit of money in five to ten years. When Linda found out about his plans, she hesitated to invest their money.

But Jerry thought, "What would she know anyway?" and signed the contract in spite of her objections.

Sometime later when he wanted to sell the land for quick money to invest in a better project, he found it was as slow to sell as Grandpa and his cane. Jerry and Linda will probably still have it when they are ready to retire. If Jerry had consulted Linda, not only would he have saved a great deal of money, but he could have given her self-esteem a boost.

We husbands would do well to remember that every one has a different stress-tolerance level. When you ignore your wife in making decisions, you add stress to every area of her life. As I've said before, stress will definitely take it's toll by eroding her physical health.

Like every other aspect of my marriage, I had to discover this the hard way. As I mentioned earlier, when my work load demanded that I travel a great deal, I didn't ask Norma if she could handle three small children alone, I just assumed she could. As a result of the extra pressure, she came to me on the verge of a physical collapse. I had to take a less responsible position in my company, but I learned the importance of taking care of my family. They bring me much more joy and fulfillment than any job. Today I can enjoy my work more because my family is always beside me. I believe when a man learns to enjoy his family above all else, his activities and his friends take on an even greater meaning as well.

I look back on the past with grief when I think of incidents like the following: Norma and the children were to pick me up at work at 5 p.m. to go for hamburgers. Just as she drove up, I was called to a last-minute staff meeting. I explained quickly that I would join her in a few minutes. Instead, the meeting lasted two hours. I wasn't apologetic, though. I was angry because she had not waited lovingly and patiently for me in the car while appeasing our three hungry children.

If I could relive that experience I would take a different route entirely. I would say, "Honey, they just called an unexpected meeting. Would you like to go back home and wait for me and feed the children?" Or I would explain to my associates I had a previous commitment to my family.

Finally, arguments are probably the most common side effect of male-dominated decisions. As anger sharpens the tongue, turning it into a fierce weapon, husbands and wives can end discussions by attacking each other's character. Words spoken during the heat of an argument are sometimes never forgotten. My wife can still remember ugly things I said when we were dating.

If a woman feels threatened during a discussion, she may become angry and demand her way. If her husband doesn't understand she is acting that way because he threatened her security, he may feel his ego is being attacked or his leadership questioned. And both will pursue the issue like wild dogs, fighting to be the leader of the pack. At any point in the discussion, either could enter the other person's world to understand why they are so upset.

Suppose a husband who is having difficulties with his wife comes up with the idea of taking a short vacation for a few days to better their relationship, while leaving the kids with Grandma. His wife may say, "You're pressuring me." He feels like he has been verbally slapped in the face. He wasn't trying to pressure her and furthermore, he sees no logical reason *why* she should feel that way. Tempers flare, and argument # 1,241 begins. But who's counting? The point is, if a woman says she feels pressured, take her word for it — *SHE FEELS PRESSURED*! Try to enter her world to discover why she feels that way — don't argue that you didn't intentionally try to pressure her. If your idea somehow caused her to say she felt *pressured*, then she was *pressured*.

Try something like, "Honey, thank you for expressing how you felt about the vacation. I didn't intend to make you feel that way, but I can sure understand. I'll back off and maybe we can figure something else out that will meet both our needs."

The brief chart below gives an example of how to eliminate trivial arguments before they snowball into major flareups.

If she says...	Typical response from a husband	Possible statements to to build a oneness with your wife
1. "You're putting pressure on me."	"I'm not pressuring you, I just wanted to do something so the two of us could be together. Don't accuse me of that."	"Honey, I can sure understand that you're pressured. If you feel what I'm saying is pressing you, then I can sure accept that. That's not my intent, but I can understand that you feel that way. Can you share at this time any of the reasons why you feel that way?"
2. "I hate going to the beach. I don't want to go."	"That's not true. You used to like the beach before we were married."	"I know I should know why you don't want to go to the beach, but could you tell me just once more some of the reasons why you don't?"

She may have several reasons, one being that she is embarrassed about her figure. At that point a husband needs to be very tender, understanding and gentle. Remember, some women do not feel as relaxed in a bathing suit as men do.

| 3. "No, I don't want to go to the ball game with you. I hate those ball games." | "I try to do things with you. The least you could do is to go with me once in a while and support me in something that I enjoy doing." | "Honey, is one of the reasons that you don't like to go because I ignore you so much when I'm at a ball game?" |

If she says "Yes" to that question, ask her for other reasons she resists going to a game. (Remember, if you react negatively to her reasons, she'll be less willing to share her true feelings with you in the future.) You may need to give her "room to breathe" and come back at a time when she doesn't have so many things on her mind.

HOW TO MAKE DECISIONS TOGETHER

Once you have found a method that works, stick to it. Whenever my wife and I try to take shortcuts, we get into trouble. After a quick discussion about moving to the country, we located the home of our dreams. I wrote an ad for the paper to sell our home and bought "For Sale" signs to put in the front yard. A neighbor walked across the street to ask how much I was asking for our house. When I quoted the price, he said it was far too low; it might reduce the market value of other houses in the neighborhood.

A vague uneasiness began to gnaw at me. Since Norma and I had not discussed every detail of this upcoming move, I tried to call her but couldn't reach her. I cancelled the ad and plucked the sign out of the yard. When Norma finally arrived home, we filled out the chart we usually use for major decisions and decided after weighing advantages and disadvantages, it was not a good idea for us to sell our home at that time.

The simple chart we use helps us reach total agreement on

important decisions. We first list all of the reasons, pro and con, for doing something. Second, we list all the reasons, pro and con, for *not* doing it. Third, we evaluate each reason. Will the decision have lasting effects. Is the reason selfish, or will it help others? Finally, we total the pros and cons and see which wins, not who wins. Although you may think you have all the reasons you need to make the decision in your mind, seeing them ranked in black and white simplifies and streamlines the decision.

The chart forces us as a couple to consider as many facts as possible. For instance, if I am counseling someone, I find I usually cannot help them until I know plenty of facts about their unique situation. The fewer the facts, the foggier a situation appears. But on the contrary, the more facts I have, the clearer the picture and the easier the solution. Many times, if I ask a person to write down all the facts on a piece of paper, he can come up with the solution on his own.

Let me give you an example of how the chart works for my family:

EXAMPLE #1: A MAJOR DECISION — SHOULD I MOVE A THOUSAND MILES AWAY AND TAKE A JOB WITH LESS PAY?

I'll only put down a few of the reasons we used for purposes of illustration.

1. List all the reasons pro and con for changing jobs and taking my family a thousand miles away.

IF WE MOVE

What we will gain (Pro)	What we will lose (Con)
1. We will be able to raise our family in a smaller town.	1. We will be taking a cut in pay. Could we adjust to that?
2. We will gain a greater opportunity to help	2. Do we really want to live in a small town and lose all the

families in a concentrated way.

3. There are many more camping spots where we're moving and the weather is warmer year around.

4. Two of our best friends live in that town.

conveniences of a major city with nice shopping centers?

3. We'll have to move away from our friends that we love so much.

4. Can we afford to buy our own home?

5. There's not a major airport for convenient travel to my Family Workshops.

2. List all of the reasons pro and con for *not* moving my family to a new location and a new job.

IF WE STAY

What we will gain (Pro)

1. We will maintain our present salary.
2. Our children will be educated at a private school.
3. We will continue to use all the shops and stores that we know so well.
4. We will continue all the contacts we have for buying various items at discount.

What we will lose (Con)

1. We will lose our opportunity to help families on a personal and consistent basis.
2. We will lose the opportunity for our children to live in a warmer climate with a greater opportunity for involvement in sports and activities.
3. We'll lose our chance to join a church that we as a family really enjoy attending together.
4. We will lose our opportunity as husband and wife to work on our life goals together.

It's important to list reasons pro and con, both for *doing* something and *not doing* something. It forces us to think of different aspects of both viewpoints.

3. Evaluate each of the reasons given in #1 and #2.
4. Total the evaluations of each of the pros and cons for #1 and #2.

"Vote YES on the big Move," Kari's sign read. She had plastered signs all over the house to gain votes in favor of our move to another state. Like a campaign manager, she actively tried to get our other two children to cast their votes for her side.

When "voting day" came, I passed out a "ballot" to each family member. The suspense mounted as I read each vote aloud until finally the votes were tallied. The "Yes" side won unanimously.

The doctrine of majority rule doesn't apply here. If one member had voted "No," I believe it would have been important to consider *why* that member voted differently. An essential secret to a happy family is total agreement. Discussion should stay open until everyone can agree when possible. Creative alternatives can be considered when it looks as though one member is going to "hang the jury."

What to do if husband and wife are deadlocked on an important decision.
Instead of looking for a referee for the ensuing battle when a husband and wife simply cannot agree, postpone the decision as long as possible in order to gather additional facts. If it comes down to the "wire", they need to decide what is best for the family. If they still can't agree but the wife allows her husband to decide, he should make his decision with the *family's* best interest in mind. A loving, understanding attitude can melt a wife's heart and give her the security she so desperately wants in times of difficult decisions.

A successful marriage
. . .it's easier than you
think

When I was newly married, I often asked others what were the secrets of a happy marriage. They would usually say, "You and your wife will have problems, but if it's meant to be, you'll stay together. If not you'll separate." When I worried about staying close to my children, people would answer, "Your teenagers will rebel. It's just normal."

These philosophies seemed so pessimistic that I became discouraged whenever our domestic harmony was threatened during an argument. I couldn't find any articles or books written on how to become a warm loving family.

However today, I can say without reservation that several successful families have taught me a principle that made my wife become my best friend. Practicing this principle has eliminated any significant disharmony in my family and drawn us all closer. I learned this principle by interviewing more than thirty close-knit couples across the nation. Their children, even though many were teenagers, all seemed to be close to Mom and Dad and happy about it. They were enthusiastic families, even radiantly happy in most cases.

When I spoke to different groups I would scan the audience, looking for the family that seemed the happiest to interview afterwards. I often talked to the wife alone, then the husband, and finally the children. I always asked them the same question, "What do you believe is the main reason you're all so close and happy as a family?" Without exception, each member of each family gave the same answer, "We do a lot of things together." Even more amazing to me was that all the families had *one particular activity in common*, which we will discuss later in this chapter.

I can truthfully say I have tested the suggestions of these families enough to prove they are valid. I no longer fear my family will break up. Nor do I fear my children will reject my wife and me as they grow older. That's because my family is practicing the things those other successful families suggested. Let's condense their suggestions into three main factors that can draw your family closer.

THREE IMPORTANT FACTORS IN BECOMING A CLOSE-KNIT FAMILY

1. *Each of these families stressed the importance of shared activities.*

Since every family specifically mentioned *camping*, I looked into it as a possible recreational activity. Norma's first thought was of bugs and snakes and dirt and all sorts of creepy-crawlers. She didn't like camping. Though I had been camping only a few times, I couldn't remember having any insurmountable problems. We decided to give it a try. Norma reluctantly agreed, frantically clutching a can of insect repellent and stuffing mosquito coils into her purse.

We borrowed a pop-tent camper and headed to Florida. We found a beautiful campsite in Kentucky, and though I was nervous being all alone in the woods, I didn't say anything. After we parked next to the only bright streetlight within fifty feet of the showers, we built a campfire to roast hotdogs and marshmallows. It was peaceful. No one was around to distract us. We put the children to bed about nine and my wife and I stayed up to enjoy a romantic evening. A distant thunderstorm entertained us with a light show as we enjoyed a warm breeze. Though the lightning came closer and closer, we thought it was passing to one side of us and went to bed with light hearts.

The children were asleep as I crawled into a tiny little bed with Greg, and Norma joined Kari. We were lying close enough to touch hands while we whispered softly. I thought, "Boy, this is really the life. I can see why everybody likes to camp." But my feeling of serenity was blasted away as the storm began to lash furiously around us and knocked out the streetlight beside our tent. It was pitch-black except for the frequent jagged streaks illuminating the sky. Thunder rumbled, shaking the ground beneath us and the wind began to howl. Rain beat against our tent until the water forced its way through, soaking our pillows.

"Honey, do you think this camper is going to blow over?" Norma asked faintly.

"No, not a chance," I said. I really thought the camper was going to *blow up*. I knew we were going to die. But within an hour, the storm's wrath cooled enough to let the stars shine through again. We lay there breathlessly on our soaked pillows, each wondering silently whether camping was the life for us.

During the subsequent years, I was curious as to why camping plays such an important part in drawing families together. Of course, any family that faced sure death together and survived would be closer.

Colorado was the destination for our first trip in our own trailer. We could hardly wait to experience the beauty of snow-capped peaks and sniff the aroma of pine trees. I could already hear the sizzle of rainbow trout frying in the pan. As we started up the mountain, my station wagon slowed from 50 miles per hour to 30, then to 25, then to 20 until we finally slowed to the pace of 15 miles per hour. "Hot" read the temperature gauge. I felt like I was wired to the engine because my palms were sweating. Our children sensed the tension in the air and became hyper and loud.

"I've got to stop at the next pull-off area," I told them. My nerves were frayed as I pulled over. All three kids jumped out immediately. I hadn't even had time to worry about my overheated car before our youngest, Michael, screamed at the top of his lungs.

His older brother, relieving some pent-up energy, had kicked what he thought to be an empty can. Unfortunately, it was half-full of transmission fluid. The can had landed upside down on Michael's head and he was covered from head to toe, a terribly unhappy little boy. His nose, his ears, even his mouth were dripping with it. Not expecting such a calamity, we had no water in the trailer to clean him up.

We worried that he had injured his eyes because he blinked rapidly the rest of the trip.

I've mentioned only the tragic times of our camping experiences, but we've also had tremendous experiences hiking to tops of mountains and exploring the out-of-doors. But the real significance of camping will be understood, I believe, when we get to the third point discussed later in the chapter.

Doing things with your family may cost you a little extra money, but it's worth every penny.

For example, Norma called one day to ask if I would like to buy a water-skiing boat and equipment. Though I was unsure at first, the idea seemed to appeal to everyone in my family. We purchased an "extremely experienced" model. When we were bouncing across the lake, on our first time out, I noticed my wife holding on to the side as if she feared we would capsize at any moment. I thought I had everything under control, yet panic was clearly written on her face. She gripped the windshield with one hand while the other had a death grip on the bar beside her. "Norma, what's wrong?" I questioned.

"I hate boats," she said slowly.

"You've got to be kidding. You hate boats? You're the one who called me up and said you wanted to buy the boat and now you're telling me you hate boats? Would you like to explain that?"

I slowed our speed and let the boat idle so she could relax enough to talk to me.

"All my life I've been afraid of boats," she said. "I've just always had a real problem with boats." I sat there in total bewilderment.

She labored to explain that she hated boats, but she knew she could learn to like them. She enjoys them much more now, further convinced that boating and skiing will knit our lives together. She determined to endure boating long enough to learn to like it for the family's sake.

Not long after our first boating experience, I sat next to an executive of the Boeing Aircraft Corp. on a flight to Seattle. When I asked him about his family, he told me they were very close.

"What is the most important thing that holds your family together?" I asked.

"Several years ago," he said, "we purchased a yacht and as a family we traveled around the various inlets and islands in the Seattle area. My family enjoys boating so much that it has provided a tremendous way to knit us together."

I wish all fathers felt that way, but one sadly admitted when he and his children meet for a rare get-together they hardly have a thing in common.

"It's a sickening experience," he said, "to have your children back home for a visit and you have nothing in common. You know, the only thing that I can remember we ever laugh about as a family is the one time we took a three-week vacation. We rented a tent and camped. What a vacation! We still laugh about those experiences."

He didn't have any other fond memories of family togetherness. His wife had her women's clubs; he had his men's clubs; the children had their activities, and they all grew apart in separate worlds.

"Now that my wife and I are alone, we have very little in common," he lamented. "We are both two lonely people lost in our five bedroom house."

The simple principle of sharing life together has permeated every area of our family life, from supporting Greg and Michael in soccer to supporting Kari and Greg in piano. As much as possible, we look for ways to spend time together. . .cooking, fishing, putting the kids to bed, gardening. . .Everything we do as a family assures me of our unity later in life. Speaking of doing things together, I'll get back to you right after my son's soccer game. . .

When I think of a trip to Hawaii, I envision snorkeling, scuba diving, spear fishing, or anything related to being in the water. My wife thinks of an orchid lei as she steps off the airplane, dining in romantic restaurants, renting a car and sightseeing during the day. Our desires are completely different. We feel that although a husband and wife both need time to enjoy separate activities, they also need to step into the world of their mates to taste each other's interests.

While my wife is shopping, I might be snorkeling, but at night we would dine together in a very romantic place. At times my wife would want to snorkel with me, and I would enjoy sight-seeing with her. I'm not saying that I would rather be touring than snorkeling or that she would rather slip on a wet suit instead of a new dress, but we believe it is important to compromise in order to share experiences. Afterwards, when the trip is only a motel receipt in your wallet, it's experiences you shared during the trip that will draw you together.

I often ask couples if they ever do things together. When I ask about vacations and the husband's face lights up while his wife grimaces, I usually conclude they took their vacation at the husband's chosen site. It was probably a dream to him and sheer torture for her and the children.

Consider the following suggestions before planning a family outing.

First, find out what activities you and your wife would like to do together. Next, consider everyone's schedule to see if the planned outing will force hardship on anyone involved. We agreed as a family that Greg should not be involved in group sports until this season because we felt we should be camping on weekends instead of sitting on bleachers watching one member play football. From time to time, we adjust our schedule to make sure our family activities are not forcing one member to miss an important event.

At this point, ask your wife to name ten activities she would enjoy doing with you throughout the year.

1._____
2._____
3._____
4._____
5._____
6._____
7._____
8._____
9._____
10._____

Next, ask her to rate which activity of the ten is the most important to her. Don't be surprised if she prefers doing some things alone, or if she doesn't enjoy being with you at all. If she has no desire to share activities with you, reflect on your attitude toward her in the past. Have you been critical or bored? Did you pout when you had to do something she wanted to do? If so, she will remember those times and tend to avoid involvement with you in the future.

Let's go on to the second way of becoming a close knit family.

2. *Recognize everyone's need to belong.*
You and I know the good feeling we have when we're able to say, "I belong to this club." "These are my friends," or "The club needs my help."

During an interview with a pro-football cheerleader, I learned how much wives need to feel that sense of belonging. She told me she loved the way her husband treated her when she returned from a two-day trip. He was so excited to have her home. He pampered her, telling her how much he had missed her. But his appreciative attitude usually wore off in about two days. Then he would start taking her for granted again.

Why do we sit glued to the television as though our wives didn't exist? It seems we realize our love for them most when they're out of our lives for a few days. But after we've had them for awhile, the "ho-hums" set in, don't they?

The principle of belonging is powerfully illustrated by an experience I had with my daughter. When Kari was nine years old, I sensed an undefined barrier between us. I couldn't detect anything specific. We just weren't close. I didn't enjoy being with her, and she didn't enjoy me either. No matter how hard I tried, I couldn't break through the barrier. From time to time, Norma would comment that I preferred my sons over her. I said, "One of the reasons is because the boys are more responsive to me."

"You'd better do something to strengthen the relationship now," Norma said, "because when Kari gets older it will be much harder. So, I tested the value of belonging and decided to take Kari with me on my next seven-day business trip. Though we still weren't close, she became excited as we planned what to do and where to stay. During the plane trip we worked on her multiplication problems until it almost drove me crazy. . .and the man in front of us. We stayed with a farm family in Washington the first night. I noticed the rapport Kari and I felt as we laughed and sang around the dinner table with their numerous children; we were actually enjoying one another's company. At times we didn't even talk. It seemed enough just to be together. Kari seemed to have just as much fun in that farm home as she did helping me with my meetings. I let her distribute some of the material so she really felt she was a special part of my team. And she was.

We decided to take the scenic route from Portland to Seattle. I wanted to show her the small "poke and plum" town near Portland where I was raised. It's so small that by the time you "poke" your head out of the window you're "plum" out of the town. After we had a flat tire near the Columbia River, we changed it together and then walked down to the river to gather driftwood for mementos. We tried to make it up a snow-covered mountain, but had to turn around and go all the way back to Seattle the long way. We will both remember that trip, good times and bad, and especially "6 x 8".

I have *never* sensed a barrier between us in the four years since that trip. I feel a complete harmony and oneness in her company. She still has the piece of driftwood sitting on her bedroom window stand, a silent reminder of our bond.

3. *Hard times can draw a family close together.*
Foxholes make lasting friendships. Haven't you heard the stories of buddies who shared the same foxhole during wartime? Whenever they meet, an instant camaraderie that no one can ever take away from them, a feeling born from surviving a struggle together.

Families have foxholes too. Even when a crisis inflicts deep scars, the dilemma can draw the family closer.

Maybe it's the crises in camping that have such a unifying effect on a family. Any family that can survive bugs, poison ivy, storms, burnt sausage, and sand in the eggs has got to come out of the ordeal closer. During a crisis, you have only each other to rely on. We all look back on the mishaps that occurred during our trips and *laugh* though it wasn't a bit funny at the time. Like the night

Norma awakened me at two in the morning so cold that she asked, "Honey, could you take us home?" Though we were two hours from home, I abandoned my cozy bed to pack and leave. She called me her John Wayne on the way home, but at the time I didn't feel much like The Duke.

Our camping fiascos have been numerous. "Only two more hours and home sweet home" I thought after our first camping trip. Tension electrified the air as we longed to be home to hot water and familiar beds once again. Unfortunately Greg convinced us at the roadside restaurant he needed a toy that shot little plastic darts tipped with rubber suction cups. We hoped it would keep him occupied for the rest of the drive. We should have known better. No sooner did he take it out of the package, when he removed all the rubber tips from the darts. When he tried to hit a target in the backseat, he aimed too high and hit Norma on the side of the head. I cannot describe the bedlam that erupted in our car. Let me understate it by saying that it was enough for me to stop the car, calm the family, and save Greg from certain death by choking. Now when we look back on the experience we laugh, and our laughter binds us together as husband and wife and parents and children.

THE ONE ACTIVITY THAT WIVES ENJOY THE MOST WITH THEIR HUSBANDS

Many women have told me about the importance of intimate communication with their husbands — after the children are in bed, during the day on the telephone, at breakfast, at dinner, at a restaurant over a cup of coffee. These special sharing times can be the most enjoyable part of a woman's day.

My wife agrees that an intimate sharing time with me is the one thing she enjoys most about our relationship. We make it a point to have breakfast together as often as possible at a nearby restaurant to talk about the coming days. I ask her questions about what she needs for the week and what I can do to help her and vice versa. I enjoy our discussions because I know she enjoys them, but more importantly, I would really miss those times of intimate communication if we ever neglected them.

To really understand each other during our conversations, we use a concept seldom taught in the classroom. It's called the "revolving method" of communication. Though it's very simple, you'll find it a tremendous help in avoiding misunderstandings. It involves four steps:

1) I ask my wife to share her feelings or thoughts with me.
2) I respond by rephrasing what I think she said.
3) She answers either yes or no.
4) If she answers no, I continue to rephrase what I think she said until I get a "yes" response.

(My wife goes through the same four steps when I am explaining my feelings to her.)

We find our communication is more meaningful since neither of us *assumes* we automatically know what the other is saying. Misunderstandings over implied meanings have confused and ruined more discussions than you can imagine. This process has nearly eliminated misinterpretations in my marriage.

11

So you want a perfect wife

"If you were more submissive to me we wouldn't have near as many problems," I used to say to my wife in a holier-than-thou voice. I was sure we would have a harmonious and fulfilling marriage if only I could motivate her to change her attitudes and responses toward me. And I was always thinking of new, creative fool-proof ways to make her change. Of course, my creative ideas usually just made her more resistant, but I didn't let that deter me. After all, most, if not all, our problems were her fault, I thought.

I even said things like, "You're so stubborn and strong-willed you're causing our marriage to decline, to deteriorate."

Or, "If only you wouldn't get so hysterical when we discuss our future plans, I would be more willing to share my life with you. I just can't tolerate your emotionalism."

I believed, at the time, that the husband was the "captain" of his ship. When I gave the orders, I expected everyone to "snap to" and follow my leadership without resistance. My distorted view made me continually critical of my wife's behavior. I can remember threatening her to emphasize the importance of what I was saying. I gave her the silent treatment, clamming up, hoping to gain her attention so she would come crawling to me after seeing the error of her ways. And I can easily recall my persistence in lecturing her over and over again on the same issues.

Lecturing is not nearly as effective as the next three approaches:

1. *Become a consistent example of what you want her to be.*
Studies have shown that a child is much more likely to copy his
parents' actions instead of their words. I have found the same
principle true in adult relationships. A wife is subconsciously
much more willing to emulate her husband's attitudes if they have
a good relationship and she admires him. Unfortunately, the
converse is true also. The more a husband demands his wife to
change when he isn't a good example himself, the less desirous
she is to improve herself.

I tried to change my wife in a certain area for months. I bribed
her, embarrassed her, threatened not to take her on vacations,
endeavoring in many "creative" ways to make her change. But the
more I talked, the less she seemed to hear. I finally realized how
unloving my attitude had been. I told myself I would not say
another word to her about her problems until I could control
myself enough to change into the tender and loving husband she
needed.

> HOW CAN A MAN EXPECT HIS WIFE TO GAIN
> SELF-CONTROL IN AREAS OF HER LIFE
> WHEN HE DOES NOT HAVE IT IN HIS OWN?

Now *I* was ready to do some changing. "Norma, I've been
thinking of trying to change, and I'm ready to start. I'm going to
get off your back."

"You know," she said, "I've really been doing some thinking
myself, and I really do want to change, especially in that one area
that bothers you."

"No, no," I said, "don't do that, because I want to be the first to
change. If you change, I won't have as much incentive — you
know how competitive I am."

"No, Honey, I really want to try harder and I'm going to
change," she replied.

I was so confused because this was the first time she had *ever*
been interested in changing. *Then she said something I will never
forget.*

"Gary, you know one of the reasons why it's been so hard for
me to break some of my habits? It's because your attitude was so
terrible. When you criticized me, I lost all desire and energy to try.

And you are so hateful about criticizing me that I don't want to improve because it would reinforce your stinky attitudes."

Now that I had taken the pressure off of her to improve, she told me she could sense the difference in my attitude. "Gary, I really want to change and you're really helping me now."

THE FUTILITY OF LECTURING YOUR WIFE

I learned that a husband's tender, sensitive and understanding attitude creates far more desire within a wife than almost anything else he can do. Unfortunately, I hadn't learned the quality of sensitivity during our early years and my wife did not always feel free to be completely honest with me for fear of my reactions.

A cold chill runs through me when I remember how much it hurt our marriage for Norma to feel she couldn't tell me her true feelings. One of our most painful experiences in this area began at a family reunion.

We were both tired and irritated after a long day at a family get-together near Lake Tahoe when a disagreement began. I don't know how we found enough energy to have such a fight, but it flared quite easily into an argument. I became more irritated and disturbed when she repeatedly refused to submit to me about my change of schedules. Finally her attitude bugged me so much that I told her I had had it. Here I was, on the staff of an organization that taught others how to have family harmony, and I couldn't even achieve it in my own family. I lived with an uneasy feeling that Norma might blow up at the wrong time and embarrass me. I didn't want that pressure any more, so I decided I had no choice but to quit my job and try a different type of work.

We were both so angry that evening we didn't speak. I awakened at five the next morning with a sick feeling in the pit of my stomach and walked down to the lake to think. I thought through what I would say to my boss and how I would handle the changes about to happen in my life. With a degree of peace, I walked back to the motel to tell Norma of my plans.

She began to cry, begging me not to quit my job. "I was wrong," she sobbed. "I'll change."

Her immediate change in attitude confused me.

"This time you can trust me because I guarantee you this will never happen again as long as we live," she said, still crying. "I really don't want you to quit your job because you will blame me the rest of our lives. Anything you tell me to do, I will do it."

"At last," I thought, "she is beginning to see the error of her ways and now we can get down to the business of developing a more harmonious marriage."

I couldn't have been further from the truth. Norma had not been completely honest with me. Instead of a change of mind, she was so hurt and offended inside by my critical attitude that her heart had hardened. But since I was threatening her security, to take her away from friends and a home she loved, to move to a different location with no promise we'd even have any money, she hid her true feelings. At that time, I didn't understand how devastating such a threat could be to a woman. Norma fought to save her home the only way she knew — by giving in to me. But it wasn't because she suddenly understood my theory of marriage, it was simply that she had no other alternative.

She harbored those resentful feelings for years. Consequently, our relationship could not become what it should have because of her unspoken resentment toward me. She can remember hating me on the inside, but smiling on the outside. It makes me shudder to think about it. Since she appeared happy on the surface, I couldn't sense that she was inwardly disgusted with me.

As I look back on the experience today, I realize where I was at fault. I was demanding and insensitive to her needs. I made no effort to understand her physical and emotional limitations and how sudden changes affect a woman. I was also very critical of her attitudes and her fatigue. I threatened her security in a cold, calculating way. Had I been understanding enough to have waited a day or two to discuss what I wanted to do, the outcome might have been different. Only in the last few years have we developed the kind of relationship that allows this type of honesty.

2. Don't demand, share how you feel.
The second way to increase your wife's desire to improve your marriage is to *share* how you feel instead of demanding that she improve.

Let me clarify the "sharing" principle by breaking it down into four parts.

A. Learn to express your feelings through loving attitudes: warmth, empathy and sincerity. Loving attitudes dramatically increase a woman's desire to hear our comments. Warmth is the friendly acceptance of a person, the feeling that a person is important enough for your time and effort. Empathy is the ability to understand and identify with your wife's feelings. Can you put yourself in her shoes and see the situation from her vantage point? Sincerity is showing a genuine concern for your wife both in public and at home. A comment such as, "You won't believe my old lady" gives your wife good reason to be an "old lady" when you go home.

B. Try to avoid using "you" statements when sharing your feelings. When you say to your wife, "You never clean up this house," or "You never have dinner on time," or "You always yell at the children," you will find she is apt to dig her heels in deeper to resist you. According to psychologist Dr. Jerry Day, "you" statements make her more determined to have her own way. When a husband says in anger, "Can't you ever think about my feelings for a change," she thinks, "His feelings! What about my feelings!" "You" statements seldom make your wife think about you; they usually infuriate her because she knows you're not concerned with her feelings.

C. Wait to share your feelings until your anger has subsided. When you are angry, the tone of your voice alone is likely to provoke the wrong reaction in your wife. You might even spit out words you really don't mean. While you are waiting to cool off, either remain silent or change the subject to a neutral one. If your wife asks why you are quiet, answer her honestly. Try to avoid sarcasm and say something like, "I need a little time to think this through so I can better understand my feelings." Psychologist Dr. Henry Brandt encourages a husband and wife to be honest enough to say, "I'm angry right now and to discuss our problem would be disastrous. Could we wait until I've cooled off?" By waiting, you will be able to have a discussion instead of an argument.

Replacing "you" statements with "I feel" messages after you have both cooled down is a better way to share disagreements. Here are a few examples of what I mean:

Areas Your Wife Needs to Improve	Typical "You" Statements to Avoid	Examples Of "I Feel" Messages
She doesn't respect you	"I'm sick and tired of how you talk to me. You don't respect me like you should."	Honey, you probably don't realize this, but I really feel discouraged whenever I hear you say disrespectful things to me (Plug in the statement she uses that discourages you.)
She doesn't accept you the way you are.	"You really don't understand me, do you?" "You're always trying to make me into somebody I'm not."	Honey, I don't blame you for saying a lot of the things you say to me. You're a woman and many times we're just not in the same world. *But I honestly don't understand many of the ways I offend you.* And I feel that you're not accepting me for who I am.
She is impatient with you.	"You never give me a chance. Would you get off my back and give me a break, I'm not perfect. I'm not as bad as Sarah's husband."	Honey, I think you deserve a gold medal for putting up with me, and I wish our relationship was better for your sake. I wish I was more skilled in taking care of you, but it's probably going to take me a long time to learn these new habits. Many times I lose my

| She is critical of you in front of others. | "If you criticize me one more time in front of them. . .You make me sick when you criticize me like you did tonight. If you ever say that again I will never take you to another party. You sure made a fool of me tonight, didn't you?" | desire to try when you're critical of me for not improving as fast as you wish I would. Honey, I know how much you enjoy being with your friends. Would there be some time in the near future we could talk about how I feel when we're at those parties? I hate to bring it up, but there's something you do that dampens my desire to be with our friends together. I really feel embarrassed and low when you criticize me in front of them. |

D. Last, try to abandon "I told you so" statements. No matter how it's said, if it means "I told you so" eliminate it from your vocabulary. Such statements reflect an arrogance and self-centeredness that can be harmful to your marriage. Here are some of the more typical ways of saying "I told you so":

"If you had done what I asked you to do in the first place, this wouldn't have happened!"

"I knew it, just like I thought. I only asked you to do one thing. . .I can't believe that you. . .you never listen, do you?. . . See-e-e-e-e?"

"You always have to do it your way, don't
you?. . .Well, I hope you're satisfied now."

"I'm not going to say it but. . .maybe
someday you'll learn to take my advice."

Can you think of any additional ways that you say to your wife, "I
told you so?"

1._____
2._____
3._____
4._____
5._____

If you can't think of any at the moment, ask your wife if she can
remember some of them. Norma could.

   I search out the ways I have hurt Norma's feelings and she does
the same with me. She is secure, knowing *I won't allow* her to
mistreat me. She likes to be held accountable for how she makes
me feel. I, too, believe it is important for a husband to have the
courage to share his feelings with his wife. A lion can roar and
growl but it takes a real man to say it gently. Tell her you need
comfort. Let her know you need praise. (I feel I need the same
basic treatment Norma does. If she wants me to improve as a
husband, it is essential that she know what encourages or
discourages me in the process). You are the only one who can tell
your wife what you need.

3. *Create curiosity.*
The third way to increase your wife's desire to improve comes
from the old saying, "You can lead a horse to water but you can't
make him drink." But you *can* make him drink if you put salt in
his oats. The more salt you put in his oats, the greater his thirst
and the more he drinks. The more curious you make your wife,
the more she will want to listen. This principle has been aptly
named the "Salt Principle." *Be stingy in sharing your feelings.
Don't share them with your wife until you have her full attention.*
Once you master the Salt Principle, you will be able to gain the

attention of anyone, even when they know what you are doing. Simply stated the principle is:

> NEVER COMMUNICATE YOUR FEELINGS OR INFORMATION YOU CONSIDER TO BE IMPORTANT WITHOUT FIRST CREATING A BURNING CURIOSITY WITHIN THE LISTENER.

The "Salt Principle" is so powerful that I can gain the attention of my family, even if their eyes are glued to the television. If I want my children to go to bed immediately, I can use the Salt Principle to get them there without threats, taunts or screams.

The Salt Principle is so powerful that I have gotten myself into trouble using it. During a speech to a large group, someone asked a question that made me say without thinking, "Do you realize a wife can gain six attitudes that really motivate her husband to want to improve?" The moment those words left my mouth, I realized I was in trouble. A woman's hand went up. "What are those six attitudes?" she asked. I inwardly groaned as I realized I could not discuss those six attitudes and finish the topic I had started. Lowering my head, I apologized to the audience for tantalizing their curiosity. I didn't forget this salt episode because after the meeting I was mobbed by curious ladies. I can't say I felt like Burt Reynolds, but I did have to spend an hour after the meeting explaining the six attitudes. Now if you're wondering what those six attitudes are, you can find them in the mate to this book *FOR BETTER OR FOR BEST*.

I asked the young daughter of a friend of mine who was engrossed in a Walt Disney special, "Have you ever heard what happened to this boy and girl that drove out to the country where they saw a bright light shining up on a hill?"

"No, I've never heard that," she said.

"Well, I probably shouldn't tell you because it's really a little scary and just unbelievable," I said.

"Oh really, what is it?" Her interest was aroused.

"Well, why don't we just watch TV and finish this program and then we'll start the story?" Actually I was already into the program myself.

"No, no. I'll turn the sound down and you can start the story now," she said. The salt was making her so thirsty, I had to tell a little bit of the story during each commercial. After Walt Disney was over, she ran upstairs to change into her nightgown. When I laid down next to her and her little brother to finish the story, I continued to use the "salt" principle any time I felt I was losing their interest. I'd say, "And what do you think happened next?"

Let's use four steps to illustrate how to catch your wife's attention when you want to share your feelings.

Start by clearly identifying the feeling you wish to communicate to your wife. For example, you want her to understand how discouraged you become when she corrects you in public.

Next, identify some of the areas your wife wants you to change. Perhaps your wife would like you to show affection for her by holding her hand or putting your arm around her in public.

Then, use her area of high interest salted with just a pinch of your feelings, to stimulate her curiosity. Use her high interest for affection in public and say something like, "Honey, when we're out in public or with our friends, I just want to put my arm around you and show everyone how proud I am of you. But there's something that you do occasionally that takes away my desire to hold you."

Finally, add a little more salt by asking a short question to further arouse her curiosity. Say something like, "Do you know what you do?" Or, "I probably shouldn't say anything at this time, right?" Or, "Would you be interested in hearing what it is that causes me to feel this way?" If she isn't interested by this time, try it again later. Add a larger dose of salt to your statements.

Below are four examples of how a husband can "Salt" his wife to listen to his feelings.

Area You wish your Wife would change	"Salt" statements that motivate your wife to change
1. She resists your sexual advances	Honey, do you know what really encourages me to make

our marriage better? (No). It's when I see us working together in building our marriage. (Oh, that's good). I can think of a major area that makes me feel that you're not pulling with me. (Oh, what's that?) Is now a good time to talk about it? (Yes). Well, I feel misunderstood and rejected when you don't respond to me at night. Could you tell me what's wrong? (*Be extra gentle and tender during the ensuing discussion. You may find out that she feels offended or any number of possibilities but you don't have to solve the problem in one discussion.*)

2. She monopolizes the conversation at parties

Honey, I know you want to go to their home next week but there's one thing that keeps happening when we're together that really drives me away from social gatherings in general. (Oh, what is it. . .gulp). Well, I'm not sure I can really explain it without offending you. (gulp, gulp). Do you really want to talk about it? I feel left out at parties by you. (*Ask her how both of you could balance this problem. Maybe you could talk a little more and she a little less. If you discuss a plan before going to the party, you will enhance the possibility of it being more enjoyable for both of you.*)

3. She doesn't want to talk
   when you're alone with her

Honey, here we are again, talking about improving our relationship. You still want that, don't you? The best relationship possible that we can build together? (Yes). There's one thing I don't understand that happens to us during different times of the week, and I think that it is not going to help our relationship especially after the children are out of college and married and we're all alone. (Oh, what's that?) Well, it sort of involves the quiet times when you and I are all by ourselves, and I'm really wanting to talk to you but you don't seem to have this same desire to talk with me. I'm just wondering if there's something I'm doing that I'm not aware of, because I really want to talk with you but I don't sense that same interest in you. Maybe I'm not being sensitive to your fatigue, or whatever. I'd just like to know, because I really feel left out when you don't talk to me when we're alone.

4. She nags you about household repairs

Honey, I don't blame you for doing one particular thing to me from time to time, because I'm sure I deserve it. But, when you say one thing to me it really causes me to lose interest in repairing things around the house. (Oh, what's that?) Well,

I know it has something to do with me, and I haven't been able to figure it out yet. But in the meantime, it's not helping me to want to fix things around here. (Well, what is it? Tell me.) Maybe you can help me. Would now be a good time for you to help me figure out why you do this particular thing to me. (Yes, Dear, whatever it is, let's get it out in the open and talk about it.) Well, you see Honey, I feel so demotivated when you, sometimes in irritation or in anger, tell me five times to do something and I just can't remember to do it. As much as I want to, my mind just gets occupied with other things and I just can't remember. I really want to help around the house. How can we figure out together what needs to be done to help me get these things done and help you not to nag me about them? I feel really disinterested in doing it when you're nagging me.

In summary, if a man truly wants his wife to improve and their marriage to be strengthened, he should be the example of what he wants to see in her before saying anything to her. He should be courageous enough to share his feelings and avoid accusing her by using "I feel" statements. And finally, he should use the "Salt principle" to gain her full attention before sharing his feelings.

12

Watch out — it can happen to you

"Norma, I really think you should take a couple of days away from the kids considering all you've faced during my absence, all the guests you had to entertain, the wedding shower, painting Greg's room. . .I'll get a babysitter, and you just relax. I don't think you're holding up too well." I was trying to get back to work some more on this book, and somehow it irritated me that Norma sounded nervous and looked uptight.

She said, "I didn't need that. It made me feel like you don't think I can handle things on my own."

"But I don't think you're handling yourself well," I said with a scowl and a harsh voice. "Surely writing a book involves more pressure than staying with the kids!"

"I think I am doing very well," she retorted. "But you're making me feel like I can't do it alone." She wouldn't succumb to my strong pull toward a bad argument.

Then, the light flashed before me and the principles in my book broke through my irritation. I realized I was irritated and nervous and that Norma was bearing the brunt of my insensitivity. I blew it again.

"You're right. You didn't need that. You *are* doing great. When will I ever learn?"

The next morning she came over to my hideaway motel for breakfast, and we again discussed how I had missed a chance to encourage her. My motives were to help, but my insensitive words came out of a doubt that I *really* was the kind of husband I should be. If I were the right kind of husband, maybe my wife wouldn't have to feel so nervous and run down.

"Honey, only a week and I'll be finished with both books. Please hang on. What will people think of our book if you didn't look like I was making you happy?"

Norma said she understood and she reminded me that my offensive behavior comes less and less often, that the periods of disharmony get shorter and shorter as we learn how to restore our relationship.

Why are those hard times fading away? Two reasons:

1. I *admit* my offensive ways and quickly accept the fact that I haven't arrived.
2. I *earn* her forgiveness sooner by following the ideas in Chapter Five.

(Aside from those reasons, we are *both* reaching for the best possible relationship. That helps a lot!)

*When can I relax and enjoy the fruit of my labor?
In Chapter Two, do you remember the story of the young couple who separated for a year until the husband learned how to regain his wife's affection? She couldn't live with his lazy, insensitive, dominant, selfish mannerisms.

He followed many of the principles shared in this book for five years after they reunited. She was regaining a romantic love and starting to blossom. Then he made the *big mistake! He relaxed and wanted a little return for his years of effort.* He assumed that now he could start enjoying the fruit of his labor — a "normal" marriage where only the women submit and the men lead. He slowly reverted to his old habits and attitudes: lazy, insensitive, dominant, selfish. Once again she started to lose her feelings of love for him.

Today he is starting all over again. Fortunately, this time, they both desire a better marriage and both are seeking help independently.

Building a successful marriage is a *life-long effort*.

Don't relax, and never assume that you've arrived! Pride always comes before fall!

I'm tired of starting all over again
One man couldn't stick with it. He kept forgetting some of the principles shared in this book. His wife was ready to leave him and nothing seemed to help until one day I said to him, "Jim, each time you fail to *comfort her* and lose your temper, you're back to the starting block in her mind — at that point she still wants to leave you."

"That does it," he said. "No way am I going to keep starting all over again." *And he didn't.* That was the end of his angry outbursts.

You may take great strides forward, but each time you slip, you wife may think you haven't changed a bit. Remember, it took my wife two years to believe me.

RESOURCES

Brandt, Henry, with Landrum, Phil. *I want My Marriage To Be Better*. Grand Rapids, Michigan: Zondervan Publishing House, 1976.

Collins, Gary. *How To Be A People Helper*. Santa Ana, California: Vision House Publishers, 1976.

Day, Dr. Jerry. Clinical Psycholologist in Tucson, Arizona. Ideas on stress management.

Dobson, James. *What Wives Wish Their Husbands Knew About Women*. Wheaton, Illinois: Tyndale House Publishers, Inc., 1975.

Drescher, John M. *Seven Things Children Need*. Scottdale, Pennsylvania: Herald Press, 1976.

Gothard, Bill. Director and lecturer, from the Institute in Basic Youth Conflicts. Oakbrook, Illinois.

Hardisty, Margaret. *Forever My Love*. Irvine, California: Harvest House Publishers, 1975.

Hendricks, Howard. *What You Need to Know About Premarital Counseling*. Waco, Texas: Family Life Cassettes, Word, Inc.

Hockman, Gloria. "A New Way for Families to Solve Problems Together." *Family Weekly*, July 16, 1978, p. 6.

Jones, Charles, *Life is Tremendous*. Wheaton, Illinois: Tyndale House Publishers, 1968.

LaHaye, Tim and Beverly. *The Act of Marriage*. Grand Rapids, Michigan: Zondervan Publishing House, 1970.

LaHaye, Tim. *Understanding the Male Temperament*. Old Tappan, New Jersey: Fleming H. Revell Company, 1977.

Nair, Ken. *Curriculum for Spiritual Oneness in Families*. La Habra, California: Published by Ken Nair, 1977.

Osborne, Cecil G. *The Art of Understanding Your Mate*. Grand Rapids, Michigan: Zondervan Publishing House, 1970.

Wheat, Ed. Family Physician, Springdale, Arkansas: Tapes on sex in marriage.